· I ·

Almost two hundred years ago, in Germany, a boy scratched his initials on a linden tree.

He was small for his age, with brown eyes and a head that looked too big for the rest of him. He was fifth in a family of nine children, and the oldest living son. Two and a half months after he was born, his older brother died and he was given the dead boy's name: Heinrich. The first initial, H, was two slashes and a crosspiece. He gripped the penknife tightly, trying to make the lines straight.

The next initial, S, was tricky. He knew that from experience: he had carved his initials dozens of times before, and the curves of the S were hard to control. Nevertheless, he wanted to make his mark. He started on the S of his last name.

• • •

His last name was Schliemann, and in the center of that German name is the English word *lie*. Perhaps now is as good a time as any to consider the subject of lying, because the boy Heinrich did not grow up to be a truthful man.

Few people are entirely honest. Many people lie once in a while. Heinrich Schliemann lied more often than that.

Heinrich Schliemann thought of his life as a story. He was the hero. He believed he was born under a lucky star, that he was meant to astonish the world with his adventures. From the time he was a boy—or so he said—he knew it was his destiny to dig up lost cities and find buried treasure.

And this is not impossible. It is children, after all, who dare to dream wild dreams. It is children who make up their minds that they will someday be rich and famous and that their lives will not be commonplace.

But most scholars believe that when sixty-year-old Heinrich Schliemann wrote his autobiography, he rewrote his life, giving himself the kind of childhood a hero ought to have had. Because Schliemann was an imaginative and convincing liar, it's hard to know what really happened and what he made up.

He was a man who loved stories. He loved them so much that he wanted them to be true.

. . .

THE HERO SCHLIEMANN

THE DREAMER WHO DUG FOR TROY

LAURA AMY SCHLITZ
ILLUSTRATED BY ROBERT BYRD

CANDLEWICK PRESS

Partial funding for the writing of this book was made possible
by a grant from the Park School of Baltimore through its
F. Parvin Sharpless Faculty and Curricular Advancement Program.

First paperback edition 2013

The Library of Congress has cataloged the hardcover edition as follows:
Schlitz, Laura Amy
The hero Schliemann : The dreamer who dug for Troy /
Laura Amy Schlitz ; illustrated by Robert Byrd.
p. cm.
Includes bibliographical references.
1. Schliemann, Heinrich, 1822–1890—Juvenile literature.
2. Archaeologists—Germany—Biography—Juvenile literature. 3. Excavations
(Archaeology)—Greece—History—19th century—Juvenile literature.
4. Excavations (Archaeology)—Turkey—Troy (Extinct city)—Juvenile
literature. 5. Mycenae (Extinct city)—Juvenile literature. 6. Troy (Extinct
city)—Juvenile literature. 7. Greece—Civilization—To 146 B.C.—
Juvenile literature. I. Byrd, Robert, ill. II. Title.
df212.s4s35 2006
930.1'092—dc22
[b]   2005046916

ISBN 978-0-7636-2283-1 (hardcover)
ISBN 978-0-7636-6504-3 (paperback)

18 19 20 SHD 10 9 8 7 6
Printed in Ann Arbor, MI, U.S.A.

This book was typeset in Hightower and Trade Gothic.
The illustrations were done in ink and watercolor.

Candlewick Press
99 Dover Street
Somerville, Massachusetts 02144

visit us at www.candlewick.com

For my parents, who nourished my dreams
L. A. S.

To Ginger
R. B.

Heinrich Schliemann was born in 1822. His father was a clergyman, the pastor of a little village named Ankershagen. It was his childhood home, Schliemann wrote, that awakened his love for "the mysterious and the marvelous." The little village of Ankershagen was riddled with stories. Close to the Schliemann parsonage, a wicked robber had buried his dead child in a golden cradle. "Behind our garden," Schliemann wrote, "was a pond . . . out of which a maiden was believed to rise each midnight, holding a silver bowl. . . . My faith in . . . these treasures was so great that, whenever I heard my father complain of his poverty, I always expressed my astonishment that he did not dig up the silver bowl or the golden cradle and so become rich."

Schliemann's story about these folk tales may be true—or it may not. The legends about the golden cradle and the silver bowl are authentic Ankershagen stories; Schliemann did not make them up, and he may have known of them when he was a boy. All his life he was fascinated by what lay buried: by bones and graveyards and treasure. It is also possible that Heinrich only read the stories later in his life. There were books of Ankershagen folk tales in his library when he was a man.

According to Schliemann, his love for the poet Homer also began in childhood. At the age of seven, he received a Christmas present from his father, a children's book based on Homer's epic poem *The Iliad*. Inside the book was a picture of the ancient city of Ilium, or Troy. Heinrich was much struck by the towering walls of the city. "Father," he insisted, "if such walls once existed, they cannot possibly have been completely destroyed."

Heinrich's father tried to explain to his son that the city of Troy had been burned to the ground and that no one alive knew where the city had been. But Heinrich would not listen. It was then that he decided that he would someday search the world for the lost city of Troy and dig it out of the ground.

Is the story of the Christmas gift—and what it inspired—true? Who can say? *The Iliad* is a story of courage, violence, and splendor—the kind of story that can set the imagination on fire. And a copy of the children's book *was* found in Heinrich's library when he was grown up, and Heinrich's name *was* written inside—but in the handwriting of an adult. Only one thing is certain: if seven-year-old Schliemann dreamed of finding lost Troy, his dreams were abruptly set aside. When Heinrich was nine years old, his whole world changed.

• • •

Ernst Schliemann, Heinrich's father, was a poor excuse for a man of God. He was quarrelsome and violent. He drank too much and spent large sums of money on presents for a woman who was not his wife. The people of Ankershagen suspected him of mishandling money that belonged to the church. They disapproved of him and felt sorry for his wife.

When Heinrich was nine years old, his mother died and the people of Ankershagen began to show Pastor Schliemann how they felt about him. They took to marching around the Schliemann house every Sunday, banging on pots and pans and throwing stones. The village children were no longer allowed to play with the young Schliemanns.

Heinrich felt a special grief in losing touch with a little girl who was his friend, Minna Meincke. Heinrich and Minna had vowed that one day they would marry and devote their lives to searching for treasure. In his autobiography, Heinrich wrote that no trouble in his adult life caused him as much pain as "my separation from my little bride."

Little bride? When Heinrich Schliemann was writing his autobiography, tales of childhood romance were considered very touching. The tale of Minna may have been one of Heinrich's prettiest stories. He did, however, ask Minna to marry him fifteen years later.

Heinrich's ninth year was a hard one. His mother was dead, his father was disgraced, and he was sent away to live with an uncle, who arranged for his education.

In the years that followed, Heinrich's father lost his job, and the family grew poorer. It was decided that Heinrich, as the eldest son, should leave school and earn his own living. At this time, he was fourteen years old, a slight and weedy-looking boy with a hollow chest. None of Heinrich's school reports give any hint that the schoolboy was a genius. His grades were only so-so.

He spent the next five years working for a grocer named Ernst Holtz. The work was both strenuous and dull. From five in the morning to eleven at night, Heinrich unpacked heavy barrels of goods. His muscles ached, and his mind was numb with boredom. Worst of all, he felt trapped: the future held nothing but more of the same.

It was ill health that saved him. One day he lifted a heavy cask of chicory and began to cough up blood. Coughing up blood is a symptom of tuberculosis, a deadly disease that was widespread in the 1800s. Heinrich feared that unless he found less taxing work, the disease would kill him.

And so Heinrich left the grocer's shop behind. A change of climate was often prescribed as a cure for tuberculosis, and Heinrich had an itch to travel, to escape to another land. He hastened to his father's house and begged for money to take a journey. Ernst Schliemann refused.

Heinrich made up his mind to leave Ankershagen and strike out for himself. He was not to see his childhood home for eleven years.

·II·

Heinrich's first journey took him to the German port of Hamburg. It was the beginning of a lifelong passion for traveling. Heinrich wrote: "The view of Hamburg . . . carried me off to seventh heaven. . . . I turned into a dreamer." His dream, at this point in his life, was to regain his health and to rise in the world.

Unfortunately, he couldn't find work. No one wanted an employee who coughed up blood. At last Heinrich grew so poor that he wrote to ask his uncle for help. His uncle sent money with a letter that shamed Heinrich so deeply that he promised himself: "I would never again ask a relative for aid; rather would I starve to death than beg such a man for the loan of a bread crumb."

He kept that promise. He also kept the money. Shortly afterward, he heard there was a ship sailing to

South America, and the prospect of a job in La Guaira, Venezuela. The ship's agent accepted Heinrich's application gratefully. It was not easy to find young men who were willing to travel two thousand miles to a land that was best known as a breeding ground for yellow fever.

On November 27, 1841, the ship *Dorothea* "flew like a seabird over the dark foamy waves." Heinrich was bound for South America.

But he never got there. The weather was stormy, with high winds and temperatures below zero. Around midnight on December 10, Heinrich was awakened by the captain's shouts. Waves dashed against the boat with such force that the portholes were shattered, and water gushed in. "I barely saved my life running almost naked on deck," wrote Schliemann. He lashed himself to the ship's railing so that he wouldn't be swept overboard. Snowflakes fell from the sky. He said a silent farewell to his family, prayed to God, and "gave my body over to the sharks." The ship began to sink.

Then, suddenly, Heinrich's fear was swept away. He untied himself and began to climb the rigging, determined to postpone death as long as possible. As he was climbing, the broken ship rocked and pitched, sinking deep below the waves. Heinrich grabbed hold of a floating barrel. He lost consciousness. Some hours later, he awoke and found himself on a sandbank off the Dutch coast. His body was covered with bruises and deep gashes, and two of his teeth had been knocked out—but he was alive.

Fearsome though the shipwreck was, it left Heinrich feeling optimistic. Only three men survived the wreck of the *Dorothea*. "God must have chosen me for great things," he wrote. "I felt reborn." And it is a curious fact that after his shipwreck, Heinrich was seldom troubled by ill health. He took up sea bathing. He stopped coughing up blood. Though he was a small man all his life, he was tough and hardy—and his energy was boundless.

When Heinrich Schliemann made his way from the coast to the city of Amsterdam, he was penniless. He spoke no Dutch, and he didn't know a soul in the city. Nevertheless, he decided to settle there.

He found work as a kind of grown-up errand boy, carrying messages and bills around town. He lived in an attic room—freezing cold in the winter, stiflingly hot in summer. Solitary study was his only amusement, as he could not afford to go to concerts or plays. "Friendships were made in coffee-houses," wrote Schliemann, "and since I did not visit any, I had no friend."

He spent every idle moment in study. He came to realize that he had a gift for languages. He memorized long passages from French and English novels, which he recited aloud. When he came to a hard passage, he shouted at the top of his lungs. Landlords and neighbors

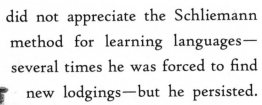

did not appreciate the Schliemann method for learning languages— several times he was forced to find new lodgings—but he persisted. He taught himself French, English, Dutch, Spanish, Italian, and Portuguese.

It must have been a lonely life, but Heinrich did not pity himself. He drew strength from his belief that he was destined for great things; he was a hero, fighting his way to fortune.

He found a better job. He became a bookkeeper for the firm of Messrs. B. H. Schröder and Company. Though Schröder and Company traded extensively with Russia, no one spoke the language. Within six weeks, Heinrich taught himself enough Russian to write letters for the firm. By 1846, he had become the Russian agent for Schröder and Company, and moved to St. Petersburg, where he was "crowned with the fullest success." Russian traders seemed to like the cocky young man who had mastered their language so quickly.

Heinrich was now twenty-four years old. Five years before, he had been a penniless nobody. Now he was a prosperous merchant, and ready to marry. He wrote to the Meincke family, only to learn that his darling Minna had already married. The older Schliemann wrote that this was "the greatest disaster" that could have befallen him.

Still, he was not altogether wretched. He loved his home in St. Petersburg. He traveled widely, going to London and Paris, Brussels, Hamburg, and Berlin. And he was earning more money all the time.

All his life, Heinrich Schliemann craved money. He never took it for granted. Even when he was a millionaire, he was stingy with small sums of money. He liked staying in grand hotels, but he always stayed on the top floor, where the rooms were cheapest: he would rather climb six flights of stairs than pay for a room lower down. He always carried his own trunk—why waste a dollar on a porter? He could not bear for anyone to cheat him.

On the other hand, he could be both generous and extravagant. He had a weakness for well-tailored clothes and spent a surprising amount of money to have his shirts regularly cleaned and starched. He was endlessly loyal to his family, sending ever-increasing amounts of money to his brothers, sisters, and father.

In 1850, Heinrich learned that his brother Ludwig had died of typhoid fever in California. Ludwig Schliemann was one of the many treasure seekers who headed to California during the Gold Rush. Heinrich went to America to settle his brother's debts and to make sure that Ludwig had a proper gravestone. Graves were always important to Heinrich—but he had another reason for going to California. Ludwig had made it clear that there were fortunes to be made in the Gold Rush. If there was money to be had, Heinrich wanted his share. Though he criticized the Californians for their "swindling," "cunning," and "immense love of money," he was their equal in every way.

One of Heinrich's oddest lies was contrived in California. In his diary, he wrote a vivid eyewitness account of the San Francisco fire, which he claimed took place in June 1851. The fire actually took place in May, when Heinrich was elsewhere. It seems that Heinrich read about the fire in the newspapers and decided to write about it as if he had been there. He wrote his version of the story on a single sheet of paper and glued it into his diary so cunningly that it looks like one of the diary pages.

This was a bizarre thing to do. He was not just showing off. Heinrich lied in his *diary*. Once again, he was changing the details of his life in order to fabricate a better story. As the hero of the story, he felt that he belonged at the Great Fire.

Heinrich's time in California was not wasted. He opened a bank and traded in gold dust. During the Gold Rush years, California was a hotbed of crime and disease. Heinrich, who was finicky about cleanliness, hated it—but he stayed in California long enough to double his fortune.

His journey home was catastrophic. When Heinrich reached the Atlantic coast of Panama, he learned that his ship had just left for Europe. There would be no other ship for weeks to come. He was stranded in a place where there was no shelter and no food.

It rained without stopping for two weeks. The land teemed with scorpions and rattlesnakes. Heinrich camped under the palm trees with 2,500 other wretched travelers. No one had dry clothes, and there was no way to kindle a fire. A few resourceful souls were able to kill monkeys, iguanas, and turtles, which had to be eaten raw. Hundreds of people died. The mosquitoes gnawed at the survivors, making sleep impossible. Heinrich wrote, "I lay more dead than alive. . . . In this horrible situation all human feeling forsook us. . . . Crimes were perpetuated among us; *crimes so terrible!* that . . . I cannot think of it without cold and trembling horror."

He never explained what the crimes were. But once again, Heinrich survived. He was alive and kicking when the next ship came. He paid for a cabin onboard without haggling over the price, gulped down beef tea, and slept in dry bedclothes for the first time in two weeks. Once again, luck had sustained him, and he sailed home to St. Petersburg with a fortune and no injury worse than a wounded leg.

·III·

When Heinrich returned to Russia, he began to think seriously about marriage. He proposed to several women, all of whom rejected him. At last his choice fell on Ekaterina Petrovna Lyshina, the daughter of a business acquaintance. Heinrich had proposed to Ekaterina before his trip to America, but she had refused him. Heinrich was not attractive to women, with his small frame and round head. During his journey, he had grown no better-looking; he had, however, become very rich. Ekaterina accepted the millionaire's proposal, and they were married.

It was a bitterly unhappy marriage. Heinrich married for love. Ekaterina married for money. Neither of them got what they wanted. Heinrich nagged and scolded his wife over every penny she spent. Ekaterina grew to hate the sight of her husband. In spite of their misery, they had three children: a son named Sergei, born in 1855, and two daughters, Natalia and Nadezhda, born in 1858 and 1861.

During the next eleven years, Heinrich made more and more money. He continued to invest in groceries and luxuries. He bought large supplies of saltpeter, brimstone, and lead to sell to the Russian military during the Crimean War. "All through the war," Heinrich admitted, "I thought of nothing but money." His greatest solace was study. When he was not increasing his fortune, he continued to teach himself languages: Slovenian, Danish, Swedish, Norwegian, Polish, Latin, and Greek.

It was Greek that led him to a new world. From the very first, his relationship with the Greek language was a love affair. He was drunk with the beauty of the words. "How is it possible for any language to be so noble!" he wondered. He filled thirty-five copybooks with exercises in Greek. He read and reread Homer's poems *The Iliad* and *The Odyssey* until he knew long sections by heart. Homer's world of heroic splendor captured his imagination so totally that he carried the books with him wherever he went.

Heinrich began to tire of business. In his exercise books, he wrote, "I cannot remain a merchant any longer." And: "How is it that I who have made three fortunes am so miserably unhappy?"

The decision to give up business was not an easy one. His success in the marketplace assured him that he was worthwhile—a man of substance. Outside the world of business, he was a nobody once more. He would have to invent himself all over again.

He began his new life by circling the globe. He visited countries that were all but unknown to most Europeans. During his world tour, he put up with bad weather, rough roads, and nasty food, but high prices never failed to rouse his sense of outrage.

On the sea voyage from Japan to California, he wrote his first book, *China and Japan in Present Times*. Once back in Europe, he passed through London and visited the Crystal Palace Park at Sydenham. There he saw copies of Egyptian temples, stone tools from a cave in France, and life-size models of dinosaurs. The next day he prowled the halls of the British Museum, looking at antiquities from Egypt and Mesopotamia.

His growing curiosity about the ancient world was not unusual for a man of his time. Heinrich was living in an age when the general public was becoming more knowledgeable about the distant past. "Prehistory"—the study of human beings before the invention of writing—was a new science. All over fashionable Europe, the ancient world had become the latest craze.

Heinrich was attracted by this new science, though he had not yet decided to become an archaeologist. He felt torn between the worlds of business and scholarship. He enrolled in the French university, the Sorbonne, but took time away from his classes to mount guard over his fortune. When he heard about economic opportunities in the United States, he headed for America. The year was 1867, and the slaves had been freed for four years.

Once in the United States, Heinrich found him-

TIMELINE: A NEW IDEA OF HISTORY

1710 and 1748
Early excavations at Herculaneum and Pompeii. For centuries these ancient cities were hidden beneath volcanic ash. When archaeologists uncover them, the public is enchanted by the beauty of the "Pompeii style."

1822
Jean-François Champollion pu his "Letter to Monsieur Dacier explaining his new insights int Egyptian hieroglyphs. For cent people had marveled over Egy monuments—but no one had been able to read the writing walls. Now Champollion had b the code.

1800
Lord Elgin wrests the marble statues from the Parthenon, a temple sacred to the Greek goddess Athena. The statues are displayed in London and cause an artistic sensation.

self deeply moved by the ambition and intelligence of the former slaves. He wrote that any statements about the laziness of Negro freedmen were "downright falsehoods. . . . They are as willing and eager to work . . . as any workmen I have yet seen and . . . both morally and intellectually, they stand much higher than their former tyrants." He sympathized with the former slaves' struggle to create a new and a better life. He had never forgotten what it was to be an underdog.

Heinrich celebrated his forty-sixth birthday alone, in New York City. Though he did not yet realize it, he was about to set off on a heroic quest: a lifelong search for the lost city of Troy.

1854
During the famous exhibition at the Crystal Palace Park in London, life-size models of dinosaurs are put on display. Ordinary people—not just scientists—get their first glimpse of those long-ago giants.

an Jürgenson Thomsen
ʜes his "three-age" version of
ɔient world, dividing prehistory
ɛ Stone Age, the Bronze Age,
ɛ Iron Age. Since the heroes of
's *Iliad* wielded bronze weapons,
⸱lieved that the Trojan War took
Juring the Bronze Age.

1859
Charles Darwin publishes his theory of evolution. This theory refutes the accepted idea that the world was created 4,004 years before the birth of Jesus Christ. People begin to imagine a past that stretches back hundreds of thousands of years.

HEINRICH SCHLIEMANN

1. Aachen
2. Tunis
3. Alexandria
4. Bologna
5. Florence
6. Naples
7. Pompeii
8. Capri
9. Paestum
10. Marseilles
11. Paris
12. Würzburg
13. Alexandria
14. Cairo
15. Ceylon
16. Madras
17. Calcutta
18. Delhi
19. Mushoori
20. Agra
21. Lucknow
22. Mirzapoor
23. Singapore
24. Jakarta
25. Java
26. Saigon
27. Canton
28. Hong Kong
29. Shanghai
30. Tientsin
31. Peking
32. Yokohama
33. Tokyo
34. San Francisco
35. Nicaragua
36. Havana
37. Mexico City
38. London
39. Paris

·IV·

Most modern scholars think that it was not until the age of forty-six that Heinrich Schliemann made up his mind to look for Troy, the lost city of Homer's *Iliad*. Before 1868, there is nothing about finding Troy in the thousands of letters and papers written by Heinrich Schliemann. If—as Heinrich maintained later in life—he had dreamed of finding the lost city since he was seven years old, it was a dream he had never shared. It was a dream he had buried as deep as Troy itself.

And it was a peculiar dream. Most of the scholars of Schliemann's day doubted whether Troy was a real place. Homer's war poem *The Iliad* was considered the greatest epic of all time, but it was considered to be fictional, an invented tale. Troy was a place in a *story*, like Oz or Narnia or Neverland.

Heinrich, of course, wanted the story to be true. He wanted to believe that the Trojan War was a real war that happened just the way Homer said it did. If current scholarship held that Troy was a myth, the scholars were wrong. Heinrich preferred the historians of ancient Greece.

The ancient Greek writers believed that there had once been a great war between the Greeks and the Trojans. Greek historians like Thucydides (c. 460–400 BCE) and Herodotus (c. 484–425 BCE) considered the Trojan War part of their ancient history, and although they couldn't be sure exactly when it occurred, they agreed that it took place roughly eight hundred years before their time, around 1250 BCE. Greek historians came up with these dates by keeping track of family histories and stories: "Let's see, my grandfather said his grandfather said *his* grandfather said . . ." This is not the most accurate way to keep track of historic events, but the Trojan War took place before the Greeks adopted an alphabet from the Phoenicians and began to write.

The ancient Greek historians also agreed that Homer lived four to six hundred years after the Trojan War. It is most likely that Homer's two great works, *The Iliad* and *The Odyssey*, were composed orally and sung by bards. During the seventh century, the Greeks became fully literate, and different versions of the poems were tacked together and written down.

WHO WAS HOMER?

Homer was the greatest poet of the ancient world. According to tradition, he lived nearly three thousand years ago. He was said to have been blind: in ancient Greece, blind men often became storytellers. When we speak of those two astonishing poems, The Iliad and The Odyssey, we say they are "by Homer."

Homer is a mysterious figure. Everyone agrees on his genius—but no one is sure whether or not he ever lived. Some scholars think that the poems were composed by many men, over hundreds of years. Heinrich Schliemann believed in a single "Homer"—the blind poet of legend.

According to many scholars, Homer never wrote a line of poetry. During his lifetime, the Greeks had no alphabet. The great poems were created, learned by heart, and chanted aloud. This must have been a staggering feat of memorization—both The Iliad and The Odyssey are so long, it would take several days to recite them.

Homer's two masterpieces are very different. The Iliad is the tale of the warriors who fought in the Trojan War, particularly the doomed and defiant Achilles and his enemy, the noble Hector. The Odyssey, which takes place after the invasion of Troy, is an adventure story. It follows Odysseus, the craftiest of the Greek warriors, on his journey home to Ithaca.

By the time Heinrich Schliemann was born, European historians had come to question the entire existence of a poet named Homer. They even wondered whether there had been a Trojan War. Above all, they wondered how much truth could be left in a story after it had been told and retold for hundreds of years. Scholars reasoned that if there had ever been any historic truth to *The Iliad*, it had long ago been lost.

Heinrich, of course, did not reason that way. In matters that touched on Homer, Heinrich did not reason: he was ruled by his imagination and his heart. He

TIMELINE: TROY

1250 BCE
This is the date that is usually given for the Trojan War. It comes from Herodotus, the Greek historian. Other Greek historians date the war as early as 1334 BCE or as late as 1150 BCE.

650 BCE
A full text of *The I[liad]* written down. Ther[e] many versions of H[omer's] poems at this time[,] slightly different. G[reek] children study ther[e at] school, and they a[re] also recited at relig[ious] festivals.

3600 BCE
First settlements at Hissarlik. Like the Troy of Homer's *Iliad*, Hissarlik is located close to the Dardanelles. The Bronze Age inhabitants of Hissarlik are traders, shepherds, and horse breeders.

730 BCE
This is generally given as the date when Homer composes *The Iliad*, his epic poem about the Trojan War. The date is not exact—it is not even certain exactly when Homer lived.

worshiped Homer and adored *The Iliad,* and he believed that if Homer's poem sang of a city of Troy near the Dardanelles, it was a real city. If Heinrich followed the clues in Homer's poems very carefully, he might be able to find the ruins of that city and bring it to light.

Heinrich's visit to "the fatherland of my darling Homer" began in 1868, with a visit to Corfu, the Greek island where the shipwrecked Odysseus met the princess Nausikaa. In *The Odyssey,* Odysseus meets the princess by the River Cressida, where she is washing clothes

300–100 BCE
Scholars in Alexandria put together a perfect text of *The Iliad* and *The Odyssey.* The epic poems are also divided into chapters, or "books," for the first time.

1868 CE
Heinrich Schliemann visits Bunarbashi and Hissarlik. Guided by Frank Calvert and the poetry of *The Iliad,* he concludes that the mound of Hissarlik covers the buried city of Troy.

528 BCE
eign of Pisistratus, rant of Athens. ding to tradition, atus gathers the famous bards of y and orders them ite *The Iliad* and *dyssey* before s.

1796 CE
A famous scholar, F. A. Wolf, asks the "Homeric Question": Was there really a poet named Homer? How many authors were responsible for *The Iliad* and *The Odyssey*?

with her maids. Because Odysseus is naked, he holds a branch in front of his loins. Heinrich followed the same path, and suffered the same embarrassment as Homer's hero. In order to cross the river, he took off his trousers. A number of women in a nearby field stopped work long enough to have a good giggle at the German businessman in his underwear. It seems likely that Heinrich was, in a private, middle-aged way, *playing* Odysseus—and it was a good role for him. Odysseus was a crafty man, quick to invent a tale, a traveler who had been shipwrecked and stranded.

After Corfu, Heinrich followed Odysseus back to his homeland—Ithaca. Unlike Troy, Ithaca was a name that could be found on any map. *Whether* Odysseus ever lived was a matter of opinion, but there was no question as to *where* he lived: Odysseus was king of Ithaca. There were even guidebooks that gave locations for "Odysseus's palace" and other Homeric sites. Heinrich was exactly the kind of tourist for whom these books were written. He walked in his hero's footsteps and shed tears at the sites where Odysseus once wept.

He also did his first digging. He dug in the ground where folk memory placed the palace of Odysseus. Here he found five or six vases filled with ashes. Since the Greeks in Homer's poem cremated their dead and buried the ashes in vases, Heinrich's fancy took a giant leap. "It is very possible that I have in my five little vases the bodies of Odysseus and Penelope." It was his first excavation, and one that was to prove characteristic. He followed the story, delved into the earth, and leaped to ecstatic conclusions about whatever he found.

After this heady discovery, Heinrich proceeded to Mycenae, the stronghold of Agamemnon. It was said that the warrior-king of *The Iliad* lay buried there, though his tomb had never been found. Heinrich admired the famous lion-carved gates of the Mycenean kings and braved the bats in Agamemnon's treasury. He spent the next week exploring the Greek islands, before proceeding to Bunarbashi, a Turkish village near the Dardanelles.

Heinrich was not the only man in Europe who believed in a real Trojan War and a real Troy. Though he was in the minority, he was not alone. Other scholars who had considered the matter had concluded that Homer's Troy might lie beneath the village of Bunarbashi. Heinrich decided to see for himself.

From the first, Heinrich was disappointed by Bunarbashi. For one thing, it was dirty, which offended his tidy soul. For another, it was ten miles from the sea. Heinrich, who knew much of *The Iliad* by heart, remembered that the Greek warriors went back and forth from their ships to the city several times a day. If the distance between the two points was ten miles, this would be impossible. He also recalled the famous scene in *The Iliad* in which the Greek hero Achilles chased the Trojan prince Hector around the walled city. Heinrich tried to act out the chase and failed. The hill was so steep that he could get around it only by crawling on all fours. Heinrich was perplexed: *Homer could not have been mistaken about the chase.* Since Homer could not be wrong, Troy must lie on some other hill. After a cursory dig, Heinrich abandoned Bunarbashi for the plain of Hissarlik.

Heinrich was by no means the first to consider Hissarlik as a possible site for Troy. For the last hundred years, there had been scholars who suspected that Troy was at Hissarlik rather than Bunarbashi. One of these men was an archaeologist named Frank Calvert. It was Frank Calvert who first discovered that what looked like a large hill on the Turkish plain was actually a mound made by human beings. Frank Calvert believed that inside that mound lay the lost city of Troy. He bought some of the land and started digging.

BCE?
LETTERS + NUMBERS = DATES

Throughout this book, dates are given in terms of the Common Era. The "Common Era" is a new way of talking about historic dates. American and European historians have traditionally used a calendar based on Christianity. Events of ancient history—like the Trojan War—were given a "BC" after the number, meaning, "before Christ." Things that happened after the birth of Christ were labeled "AD" for "anno Domine"—Latin words for "in the year of Our Lord."

Common Era dating uses the same numbers, but different initials after the dates. What used to be called 5 BC (five years before Christ) is now called 5 BCE (five years before the Common Era.) Historians use Common Era dates as a way of being courteous to people of all religions. Common Era dates are also more accurate, since it is not certain exactly when Jesus Christ lived.

When Heinrich met Frank Calvert in 1868, he adopted Calvert's beliefs: "I completely shared Frank Calvert's conviction that the plateau of Hissarlik marks the site of ancient Troy."

Heinrich gave Hissarlik the same "tests" he had administered at Bunarbashi. He concluded that Hector and Achilles could easily have run the nine miles around this mound. He was delighted to discover a ruined temple, a nearby swamp, and a mountain range in the distance—all of which reminded him of landscapes in *The Illiad*. "The beautiful hill of Hissarlik grips one with astonishment," he wrote later. "That hill seems to be destined by nature to carry a great city." All of the clues in *The Iliad* seemed now to point to Hissarlik as the site of ancient Troy. Heinrich was so excited that he ordered a chicken dinner to celebrate. Unfortunately, the chicken who was to be the main course objected to the whole idea and ran for its life, squawking in panic. Heinrich, who had a soft spot for animals, paid the owner to set the chicken free and sat down to a poultry-free supper in high good humor.

Heinrich Schliemann is famous for "finding Troy." Many people give him credit for being the first to look for Troy in the right place—but by right, that honor belongs to Frank Calvert. If Heinrich Schliemann had not met Frank Calvert on his journey, he might never have excavated at Hissarlik. The admission "I . . . shared Frank Calvert's opinion" changed gradually to "Frank Calvert, the famous archaeologist . . . shares *my* opinion. . . ." Eventually Heinrich, who admitted that he was "a braggart and a bluffer," made the discovery sound as if it were his alone.

Frank Calvert, however, was a remarkably generous man. He must have realized that Heinrich had the energy, as well as the money, to organize a large-scale excavation. He gave Heinrich the benefit of his archaeological knowledge and explained how to get permission to dig from the Turkish government. Heinrich promised to return to Hissarlik the following year, permission in hand.

· V ·

The years 1868 and 1869 were remarkable
ones in Heinrich's life. He retired from business, appointed
himself Homer's champion, and divorced his wife.

He began to dream of a Greek bride: dark-haired,
interested in Homer, and—if possible—beautiful. He
had no desire for a rich bride. He knew he was not
handsome, and he hoped to make up for it with a well-
padded wallet and a knowledge of foreign languages. He
told his Greek tutor, Theokletos Vimpos, that he wanted
his future wife to love learning "because otherwise she
cannot love and respect me." Above all, he wished for "a
good and loving heart."

As it happened, Theokletos had an unmarried niece:
dark-haired, bookish, and poor. Sophia Engastromenos
was only sixteen years old when her photograph was
sent to the forty-seven-year-old millionaire. Her youth

frightened Heinrich. He was afraid that so young a girl would have her heart set on romance. But Sophia's photograph enchanted him, and at last he declared that he had fallen in love.

Having fallen in love with Sophia, it only remained to meet her. The Engastromenos family was excited by the prospect of having a millionaire in the family, and Sophia was bundled into her sister's best dress. When Heinrich spoke to her alone, he asked her point-blank, "Why do you wish to marry me?" Sophia replied, "Because my parents have told me that you are a rich man!"

Heinrich flew into a temper and marched back to his hotel room to sulk. The Engastromenos family huddled around Sophia, begging her to send a letter of apology. Sophia wrote that she had not meant to offend her suitor; she had answered honestly because she believed that he wanted the truth.

Heinrich forgave her. By this time, he was head over heels in love. For the second time in his life, he married a woman he had barely met, a woman whose family was in need of money. This time, his wife was thirty years younger than himself—Sophia was so young that she smuggled her dolls along on her honeymoon.

Poor Sophia! During the first months of married life, Heinrich dragged her to museums all over Europe. She preferred the circus. He lavished expensive gifts upon her, supervised her diet, and drew up a gymnastics program that he thought would keep her healthy. He pestered her to learn foreign languages. She suffered from headaches, stomachaches, and homesickness.

And yet the marriage was not a disaster. Sophia Schliemann was loving and wise beyond her years. She relieved Heinrich's deep loneliness. She made up her mind that "Henry" was a genius and that geniuses were not quite like other people. She even awakened a streak of playfulness in his nature—on their honeymoon in Venice, he dived headfirst out of a gondola in order to make her laugh. She called him her "friend for life" and "dearest husband."

As for "Henry," his love and respect for Sophia increased as he came to know her better. To him, she was his "adored wife and everlasting friend." He admired her mind as well as her beauty and concluded, "I knew I loved and needed a woman of her grandeur."

In 1871, Sophia gave birth to a baby girl who was christened Andromache, after the Trojan princess in *The Iliad*. Shortly after Andromache's birth, Heinrich received the *firman*, or permission, he had been seeking from the Turkish government. The terms of the agreement were simple: Heinrich was responsible for all expenses. If artifacts were found, half of them were to be given to the new museum in Constantinople. A supervisor was appointed to keep a watchful eye on the amateur archaeologist. Heinrich disliked the man and grumbled over having to pay his salary.

When Heinrich began digging at Hissarlik, he had very little idea what he was doing. He knew that he wanted to dig into the mound and find a city of the Bronze Age, but he didn't know what a Bronze Age city would look like. His guide was Homer—he was looking for artifacts and architecture that matched the descriptions in Homer's poetry. This was not a scientific approach.

The thrust of his plan was to dig—deep. At the top of the mound, he expected to find a Roman city, then a Greek city underneath, then a Greek city from the time of Homer, and, just below that, the walled city of *The Iliad*. Instead of carefully sifting through the mound, layer by layer, he decided to dig out vast trenches—rather as if he were removing slices from a cake. Since Homer's Troy was ancient, Heinrich expected to find it near the bottom.

And so he dug, violently and impatiently. Frank Calvert advised him to proceed with care, to sift through what he was throwing away, but Heinrich was not a cautious man. He whacked away at the mound as if it were a piñata.

Modern archaeologists do not dig like this. They remove the earth gently and keep detailed records of what they find. If they find an artifact that isn't what they're hoping to find, they don't discard the artifact: they change their ideas. Instead of looking *for* something, they examine whatever comes to light. Heinrich, of course, was looking for Homer's Troy. "Troy . . . was sacked twice," modern archaeologists remark, "once by the Greeks and once by Heinrich Schliemann." It is generally agreed that Schliemann did more damage than the Greeks.

His early finds were not very interesting. He discovered the remains of a wall. He found coins, a few bones, the clay whorls that women used in spinning thread. Later there were little objects made of clay, which he thought were "owl-headed" vases, sacred to Athena. He was looking for weapons like the "pitiless bronze" spears described by Homer—but the weapons he found were made of stone. Heinrich was bewildered. He was seeking the remains of a great city. Where was the bronze armor, the palaces and jewels?

Spring turned to summer. The climate of Hissarlik tends to extremes—bitter cold in winter, blistering heat in summer, and a wind that never stops blowing.

Since Homer sang of "windy Troy," Heinrich had once rejoiced that Hissarlik was windy, but his enthusiasm for high winds was waning. Gusts of air blew grit into his eyes. Dust scratched his skin and filled his mouth when he tried to speak.

As the workmen dug, they unearthed thousands of poisonous snakes. Hissarlik was also home to scorpions and mosquitoes. At night, it was difficult to sleep: there were so many shrieking owls and croaking frogs. Poisonous centipedes invaded the Schliemann bed.

The workmen grew weary of hauling heavy wheelbarrows full of earth. They began to work more slowly, frequently pausing to smoke. Heinrich badgered them about their smoking. He believed that smoking wasted time and weakened the body.

Heinrich had become an unpaid doctor. He hated dirt and disease, and could not see either without wanting to meddle. He gave the workers quinine in order to prevent malaria. He preached the virtues of exercise, fresh fruit, and sea bathing.

Heinrich was particularly proud of curing a girl of seventeen. She was almost too weak to walk, she coughed uncontrollably, and her body was covered with ulcers. Heinrich was shocked by her frailty and the filthy rags she wore. He called for castor oil and administered a dose; he also asked Sophia to give the girl a pretty dress from her own wardrobe. He taught his patient a few simple exercises and told her to take daily sea baths. A month later, she walked three miles to kiss the dusty shoes of "Dr. Schliemann." Her cough was gone, and the ulcers were healed. She was happy and strong.

Heinrich was touched by her gratitude, but—as he often complained—he had come to Hissarlik to excavate Troy, not to play doctor. He urged the workers to dig deeper, to go faster.

The first season ended. Heinrich hired more workmen. He was beginning to understand the way the mound was layered. Little by little, he came to distinguish between the ruins of four different cities—cities that lay on top and outside of another, like nesting dolls or the layers of an onion.

In an onion, however, the layers are orderly. At Hissarlik, the layers are uneven and the boundaries overlap. The site would have confounded a far more experienced archaeologist than Heinrich Schliemann. "It was an entirely new world for me," confessed Heinrich. "I had to learn everything by myself."

During the second season, Heinrich found a panel of carved marble that showed the sun god in his chariot. Though the panel, which dates from between 355 and 281 BCE, was not old enough to belong to Homer's Troy, it was the largest and most beautiful object yet found—and it was found on Frank Calvert's land.

STRATIFICATION
The Layers of History

When Heinrich Schliemann dug at Hissarlik, he was hoping to find Homer's city of Troy. Instead, he found many cities, one on top of the other. Sorting out the different layers, or strata, was a difficult job.

In order to understand Heinrich's work, imagine that you've tossed everything that you've ever owned into a heap in the middle of the floor. On top of the mound would be the clothes you wore yesterday. Lower down, the clothes would be smaller. Legos and puzzle pieces would get bigger. At the bottom of the mound would be baby clothes, board books, and rattles.

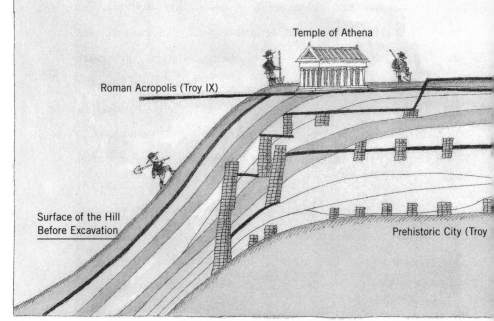

Temple of Athena

Roman Acropolis (Troy IX)

Surface of the Hill
Before Excavation

Prehistoric City (Troy

If you looked at the mound like an archaeologist, you'd see all the layers of your past life. You would keep a sharp eye out for anything that might help you to assign dates to the different strata. If, for example, you found your second-grade report card next to a plastic stegosaurus, you might guess that second grade was the year you were crazy about dinosaurs.

Now suppose your mother wanted to give away the red boots you loved when you were four. Suppose she tore apart your mound like a dog looking for a bone. What had once been an orderly mess would become chaos. The original layering, which made sense, would be lost forever.

What Heinrich Schliemann did at Hissarlik was quite a bit like that.

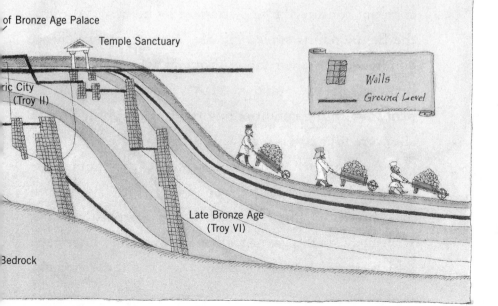

of Bronze Age Palace

Temple Sanctuary

ric City
(Troy II)

Walls
Ground Level

Late Bronze Age
(Troy VI)

Bedrock

Calvert and Schliemann had agreed that whatever was found on Calvert's section of the mound would be divided between them, but the marble panel could not be cut in half. Heinrich wanted the whole thing. He offered to pay Frank Calvert for his share of the sculpture.

It was the end of their friendship. Since their first meeting, Frank Calvert had been unstinting with his knowledge and advice. Now Heinrich haggled like the cut-throat businessman he was. He succeeded in beating down the price, but he lost Calvert's respect. Later, when Calvert published criticisms of Schliemann's theories in historical journals, Schliemann felt betrayed.

Heinrich was publishing his discoveries almost as quickly as he made them. He expected the scholars of the world to applaud his labor; instead they accused him of jumping to conclusions. Heinrich raged at the criticism but continued to dig, assisted by his wife. At night the Schliemanns stayed up late, measuring, sketching, and recording their finds. Sophia, who had been so homesick in the grand hotels of Europe, accepted the primitive living conditions without a murmur, though she wore four pairs of gloves during the winter.

As Heinrich continued to study the mound, he came to believe that the second city from the bottom was the city of Homer's *Iliad*. It was a prehistoric city, with a paved ramp, a magnificent tower, and a huge gate, which Heinrich at once assumed was the "Scaean Gate" of *The Iliad*. The walls had been skillfully constructed, and—even more important—showed signs that the city had once been burned, like Homer's Troy.

Heinrich was outwardly delighted, and inwardly puzzled, by this city. He wanted nothing more than to believe that he had found Homer's Troy, but the city was very small—only about a hundred yards across. He found bronze and copper weapons, but the pottery found at this level was oddly primitive.

And there was no treasure. By now, Heinrich had been an archaeologist long enough to understand that he was supposed to be seeking knowledge, not treasure, and he was quick to assert that his only desire was to find Troy itself. But the lack of treasure was a nagging disappointment. Homer said that Troy was "rich in gold," but Heinrich had found little that was precious.

It was not until 1873 that Heinrich found the riches his heart craved. According to Heinrich, the treasure was found on the last morning of May. He was digging into a wall when he caught a glimpse of shining gold. Some instinct told him that there was a rich treasure hidden within the wall, and he resolved to dig it out for himself. He announced to the workers that it was his birthday (it wasn't) and told them to take the day off. He summoned Sophia to his side and told her to fetch her red shawl. Together, the husband-and-wife team worked to dig the artifacts out of the wall. There were thousands of precious objects: helmets and swords, vessels of gold and silver, shields, lances, vases, cauldrons, and jewelry. There were more than eight thousand gold rings; there were earrings and brace- lets and necklaces and diadems.

Sophia bundled the treasure in her shawl and carried it back to their living quarters. Once they were alone together, Heinrich decked his beautiful wife in the golden diadem that had once kissed the brow of Helen of Troy.

This is a good story. It is still found in books, but it is not true. For one thing, Sophia Schliemann was not with her husband on May 31. Her father had recently died, and she had gone to Athens for the funeral. As early as December 1873, Heinrich admitted to a friend at the British Museum that he had made up the story of Sophia and her red shawl. He explained that Sophia was becoming a gifted archaeologist and he wanted to encourage her by including her in the story of his great discovery.

Sophia's absence is not the only thing wrong with Heinrich's account of that day. Scholars who have examined Heinrich's notes also know that some of the objects in the treasure were found earlier—he had dated and photographed them *before* May 31. In fact, Heinrich combined several finds in order to make up what he called "Priam's treasure" after King Priam in *The Iliad*. His dramatic instinct demanded that the treasure be as lavish as possible, so he added to what he found.

Heinrich had a theory—or fantasy—about the treasure, and he wanted the world to share it. According to him, the treasure was hidden on the night Troy was invaded by the Greeks. Led by the crafty Odysseus, the Greek soldiers infiltrated the city, concealed within a wooden horse. Now they attacked with fire and sword. "The treasure was packed together at terrible risk of life, and in the greatest anxiety," wrote Heinrich. For Heinrich, a well-built city, signs of fire, and a hastily hidden treasure added up to one thing: Homeric Troy. He had solved what he modestly referred to as "the greatest and most important of all historical riddles."

Heinrich told the story of how he discovered Priam's treasure many times, and he never told it the same way twice. His shiftiness about the finding of the treasure was so noticeable that some of his fellow scholars suspected him of paying artists to make the precious objects and burying them himself, only to dig them up later. "Priam's treasure," which Heinrich thought would be the greatest triumph of his career, was also the greatest scandal.

• • •

A word about the treasure: It did not belong to King Priam, and it was not worn by Helen of Troy. Though the treasure is ancient and genuine, it predates the Trojan War by a thousand years. Modern archaeologists have since divided the site at Hissarlik into at least nine different Troys, dating from nine different periods of occupation. Heinrich's prehistoric city, second from the bottom, is generally known as Troy 2. Heinrich's dating, for both the treasure and the city, was a thousand years off: Troy 2 was not Homeric Troy.

It's easy to laugh now. To be "off" by a thousand years is to be pretty far "off." It's important to remember, though, that ancient artifacts do not come out of the ground with dates on them. Modern dating methods, such as radiocarbon dating, did not exist in Heinrich's time. In Heinrich's day, archaeologists had to figure out how old objects were by keeping track of how deep they were buried and by comparing them to other objects. Because the artifacts Heinrich was finding were so ancient, he didn't have objects with which to compare them. Later on, archaeologists came to date materials by creating a sequence of styles in pottery. Though Heinrich loved gold and precious stones, he was one of the first archaeologists to realize the importance of pottery. In this, he was ahead of his time.

In falsifying details of the treasure, however, he was doing his fellow archaeologists the kind of injury they find hard to forgive. All archaeologists, past and present, work together. Each object is a clue to the past, and archaeologists count on one another to pass on only the right clues. In hedging about exactly where and when the objects were found, Heinrich cheated his colleagues of the opportunity to learn the real history of his treasure.

·VI·

Though finding "Priam's treasure" was the thrill of a lifetime, it created a dilemma for Heinrich. According to the rules of the *firman*, half of the excavated goods belonged to the Turks. Heinrich had two choices: he could surrender half the treasure, or he could keep it a secret. He could not publish his great discovery without losing half of what he had found.

Either option was more than body and soul could bear. Heinrich could not wait to dazzle the public. He believed that the Trojan gold would bring him undying glory. The temptation to publish his finds was irresistible.

On the other hand, he could not stand to part with any of the treasure. Heinrich had a childish "finders-keepers" feeling about the Trojan gold. It was his connection to Homer, something he could hold in his hands. He had borne heat and dust and ridicule for it. He could not let it go.

The solution to this problem was a crooked one. Heinrich was neither the first nor the last archaeologist to resort to it. He smuggled the treasure out of the country. No one knows exactly how he did it: he may have been helped by the Calvert brothers or by members of Sophia's family, but the finding of the treasure was kept a secret. Once the gold left Turkey, Heinrich closed down the excavation and returned to Athens. There he photographed the treasure and wrote articles about its finding.

When the articles were published, Heinrich was in trouble, as he fully deserved to be. Though Greece and Turkey had been at odds for hundreds of years, the Greek government agreed that Schliemann ought to return the treasure to the Turks. When the authorities came to claim it, the treasure had vanished again. It seems likely that Heinrich divided it among the members of the Engastromenos family, who hid it in caves and barns.

Heinrich knew that he might go to jail, but didn't care. "I kept everything valuable that I found for myself and thus saved it for science," he wrote self-righteously. Guards surrounded the house. Policemen searched his belongings. The Schliemann bank accounts were frozen. Heinrich was questioned about the whereabouts of the treasure, but he kept his mouth shut. Only once did he come close to admitting his guilt. The Turks had arrested Effendi Amin, the watchman who had been hired to keep an eye on the Schliemann excavation. Heinrich felt no shame about stealing the treasure or smuggling it out of the country, but it distressed him that Effendi Amin should be put in jail for what he had done. He wrote to the Turkish government, pointing out that the loss of the treasure was not Amin's fault—he had done his best. He begged them, "in the name of humanity" to set Amin free.

There was a long court case. Eventually the Turks gave up and agreed that Heinrich should pay them for the treasure, a fine of fifty thousand francs. He joyfully sent five times that amount and a number of artifacts he did not greatly admire. Once again, his luck had held. Perhaps Hermes, the Greek god of thieves, protected him. Against all odds, he was able to keep the Trojan gold.

He was not, however, as celebrated as he had hoped to be. Many scholars felt that more evidence was needed before Hissarlik could be renamed Troy. Others found Heinrich's theories ridiculous, his stories preposterous. Cartoons and caricatures of the Schliemanns filled the newspapers.

All his life, Heinrich Schliemann was to irritate his colleagues. Though many scholars befriended him, he also made enemies—and his enemies simply could not stand him. They were disgusted by his romanticism, his boasting, his hysterical excitement over every new idea. It rankled that a grocer turned millionaire should unearth such staggering finds. Schliemann was a shrill and vulgar little man. What right had he to come up with theories?

Three years of frustration followed. Though he had gained fame, Heinrich had failed to dazzle the scholarly world, and he could not get permission to mount another excavation—this time at Mycenae. Because Mycenae was known to be a Bronze Age site, Heinrich hoped to find weapons and pottery similar to those he had found at Hissarlik. He also hoped to find the tomb of Agamemnon, the warrior king of *The Iliad*. Unfortunately, neither the Greek nor the Turkish government had any intention of letting him dig up anything. Who can blame them?

Heinrich argued and coaxed. It did no good. At last he resorted to bribery. He spent a huge sum of money to knock down an ugly tower that blocked a view of the Parthenon. The people of Athens had hated this eyesore for centuries, but no one had ever been willing to pay to get rid of it. Heinrich was willing to foot the bill. Shortly afterward, he received permission to dig at Mycenae. The rules of this *firman* were strict. Everything he found would belong to Greece—and he was limited to digging inside the city walls.

As it happened, Heinrich *wanted* to dig within the city walls. He believed that the royal tombs would be found inside Mycenae. He owed this belief to a Greek writer named Pausanias, who visited Mycenae in the second century of the Common Era.

Of course other scholars had read Pausanias, too, but they brought more knowledge to their reading. They knew that the city of Mycenae had once possessed *two* sets of walls, one inside the other. They reasoned that the space inside the inner wall was too small to hold the tomb of a great king. If royal tombs existed, they were certain they must lie somewhere between the inner and outer walls. It is probable the Greek government gave Schliemann permission to dig within the inner city walls because there was little chance of his finding anything there.

But Heinrich's hunch turned out to be an auspicious one—he found the tombs. Quite early on, he came upon a circle of stone markers. Inside the circle were tombstones that marked the entrance to narrow tunnels, leading straight down. At the bottom of the tunnels were underground chambers—shaft graves. Pausanias had mentioned five royal tombs, and Heinrich discovered exactly five shaft graves. (There were in fact six, but Heinrich trusted Pausanias completely; after he found the fifth grave, he stopped looking.)

As Heinrich had hoped, the graves were royal tombs, and they were magnificently rich. Fifteen royal corpses were heaped with gold. The men wore gold death masks and breastplates decorated with sunbursts and rosettes. The women were adorned with gold jewelry. All around the bodies were bronze swords and daggers inlaid with gold and silver, drinking cups made of precious stones, boxes of gold and silver and ivory. Once again, Heinrich was half-mad with enthusiasm. "I have found an unparalleled treasure," he wrote. "All the museums in the world put together do not possess one fifth of it. Unfortunately nothing but the glory is mine."

The tombs of Mycenae were even more spectacular than "Priam's treasure." The artifacts were exquisite, but that was not all—many of the artifacts matched *exactly* the descriptions found in Homer's *Iliad*. Wine cups, swords, jewels, bracelets, helmets—everything was in keeping with Homer's Bronze Age world. To crown it all, one of the gold-masked warriors had died in the prime of manhood. This, Heinrich felt certain, was the hero from *The Iliad*, the murdered Agamemnon. He knelt down and kissed the gold mask. Afterward, according to a famous story,

Heinrich telegraphed the king of Greece with the words, "I have gazed upon the face of Agamemnon."

This sounds like the sort of telegram Heinrich might have sent if he had thought of it, but the words are not his. Some other romantic soul invented the tale of the telegram—for once Heinrich himself was not responsible—and it has become part of the colorful Schliemann legend.

Was the dead king Agamemnon? No. Scholars have since determined that the shaft graves date from a hundred to three hundred years *before* the Trojan War. They were, however, Bronze Age graves. Heinrich was getting closer to the Homeric world he sought, but it still eluded him.

When a triumphant Heinrich published his findings about Mycenae, he revealed a lost world. The Bronze Age, that shadowy period between 1600 and 1100 BCE, had been drawn into the spotlight. The glory of that spotlight cast a golden glow over Heinrich Schliemann. He became a celebrity.

For the second time in his career, Heinrich's finds gave rise to scholarly debate. Many scholars felt that none of the shaft graves was ancient enough to be the resting place of the legendary king. One critic even thought that the "mask of Agamemnon" was meant to be an image of Jesus Christ. Heinrich grew testy when scholars refused to accept his bearded warrior as

Agamemnon. "All right," he snapped, "let's call him Schultze!" From that moment on, the warrior king was referred to as "Schultze." Schultze's mask continues to puzzle archaeologists up to the present day. It is unique in design, and some scholars consider it a forgery.

Nevertheless, Heinrich had made two of the greatest discoveries in archaeological history. He traveled widely during the next year, relishing his newfound fame. But even as he boasted, he was nagged by doubt. In studying the Mycenaean tombs, Heinrich formed a clearer idea of what Bronze Age artifacts looked like. Unfortunately, what they *didn't* look like were the artifacts he had found at Hissarlik. If Hissarlik and Mycenae were both remnants of Homer's heroic world, why were the sites so different from each other? Why weren't the treasures more alike?

In 1878, Sophia gave birth to a little boy, and Heinrich returned home for the christening. Heinrich had planned to call his son Odysseus, but changed his mind after his triumph at Mycenae. The infant was christened Agamemnon. Heinrich laid a book against the baby's head and read his newborn son a hundred lines of Homeric verse.

Shortly after his son's birth, Heinrich decided to return to Hissarlik. He wanted to re-examine the site. He was eager to find artifacts that would confirm his "Troy" as a Bronze Age city.

He applied to the Turkish government for a *firman* and, surprisingly, got it. He was even allowed to keep one third of whatever he found. During the 1879 excavations at Hissarlik, Heinrich was accompanied by a scholar and doctor named Rudolf Virchow.

Rudolf Virchow and Heinrich had a lot in common. Both loved Homer. The two men came from working-class backgrounds and were almost exactly the same age. Virchow's powers of energy and concentration were the equal of Heinrich's—and he shared Heinrich's fascination with human bones. In disposition, however, they were different: Heinrich was hotheaded, touchy, and dreamy; Virchow was thoughtful and self-contained.

Rudolf Virchow became a sort of father figure to Heinrich. He encouraged Heinrich to observe the land around Hissarlik, to take note of animal and plant life. He taught him to keep more accurate records and to think twice before jumping to conclusions. Virchow even advised Heinrich about personal matters. He reminded him to pay attention to Sophia and gave suggestions about what to feed the infant Agamemnon. Heinrich, who was not good at listening to other people, paid attention to Dr. Virchow—except when his new friend warned him against the dangers of bathing in icy water. Heinrich suffered from chronic earaches; Virchow told him, correctly, that his sea bathing would make the earaches worse. Heinrich ignored him.

Together Virchow and Schliemann tackled the mound at Hissarlik. More precious objects were found—Heinrich was almost getting used to finding treasure—but none of the objects resembled what he had found at Mycenae. Heinrich decided to explore other Bronze Age sites. He was driven by two hungers—to learn more and to prove that his earlier theories were right.

He excavated at Orchomenus, another of the cities that Homer had described as "rich in gold." At Orchomenus, it was Sophia's turn to make a major discovery. She found a treasury room belonging to a legendary king, covered with intricate carvings of flowers and spirals. The chamber was so beautiful that the Schliemanns paid to have it restored.

At Orchomenus, Heinrich first hired Wilhelm Dörpfeld, whom later archaeologists were to call "Schliemann's greatest discovery." Dörpfeld was twenty-seven years old. He had been trained as an architect, and he had a genius for looking at ancient ruins and envisioning how they appeared long ago. Like Virchow, Dörpfeld was a good influence on Heinrich. He taught him how to excavate with care. Though he understood the science of archaeology far better than Heinrich did, Dörpfeld loved and admired the older man.

With Wilhelm Dörpfeld at his side, Heinrich set off for Tiryns, a city linked in myth with Hercules and the "warlike Diomedes" of The Iliad. Tiryns was Heinrich's third great triumph. With the help of Dörpfeld, he uncovered a majestic palace, decorated with wall paintings of Bronze Age men and women. The site yielded vast amounts of jewelry and pottery. In both size and decoration, it was the sort of palace that Heinrich had hoped to find at Hissarlik.

Heinrich was moving into his own palace around this time. He persuaded a famous architect to create a house that would celebrate Homer's heroic poetry. The "Palace of Troy" was a fantasy world, richly adorned with statues, murals, and Homeric inscriptions, "but it contained not one stick of comfortable furniture," complained his daughter Andromache.

The lack of comfort didn't bother Heinrich. Even in his sixties, he preferred to read and write standing up. Sophia and the children were forced to make the best of living in a museum. When Heinrich went away

on business, they packed a picnic basket and spread out their picnic on one of the hard mosaic floors.

Heinrich ruled over his Homeric palace like a king. He gave the servants names out of Homer and Greek mythology. He kept hens and pigeons and forbade anyone to kill them for food. No one was allowed to pluck the flowers in the garden—Heinrich had an odd theory that plants suffered when they were picked. Besides the birds, Heinrich doted on the family dog and a kitten he had rescued from Hissarlik.

During the last decade of his life, Heinrich received many visitors at his "Palace of Troy." He had grown more comfortable with people and entertained guests with kindness and generosity. He was an affectionate but demanding father, insisting that his children study hard, exercise vigorously, and speak foreign languages. His daughter Andromache wrote, "Throughout my own girlhood he would often get me up at five o'clock in the morning in winter to ride horseback five miles . . . to swim in the sea, as he himself did every day. . . .

Beneath these imperious traits Father was warmhearted and generous to a fault. He was humble, too, in his own way."

Humble? Perhaps not. When Heinrich wrote about his finds at Tiryns, he stated, "Once again the gods granted me . . . one of the most important archaeological discoveries ever made . . . from now till the end of time." Conceited though this sounds, there is truth in it. Though the palace of Tiryns is the least famous of Heinrich's three great triumphs, excavating it was a stupendous achievement. Once again, Heinrich crowed with triumph before the public, and the public responded with a mixture of catcalls and cheers.

Wilhelm Dörpfeld, who was responsible for the superb quality of the excavation work, stood in the wings, allowing Heinrich the limelight. Perhaps he understood that his time would come, that the older man would soon withdraw from the world of archaeology.

·VII·

During the last ten years of his life,
Heinrich was often tired and sick. His earaches tortured
him, and he suffered from malaria. In spite of his illness,
he continued to travel, to swim, to write, and to dig.

In 1890, he returned once more to Hissarlik. It was
his twelfth visit, and little had changed: it was still a
place of owls and scorpions, poisonous snakes, wind
and dust. On this particular visit, Heinrich did rather a
mysterious thing: he began to excavate outside the walls
of "his" Homeric Troy.

It may have been Dörpfeld's idea. Or it may have
been Heinrich's—he had always been haunted by the
fact that his prehistoric city was so small. In any event,
once the two men dug outside the boundaries of what
Heinrich had claimed was Troy, they came upon two
buildings similar to the Bronze Age palace at Tiryns.

Inside, at last, they found what Heinrich had been looking for: pottery similar to that he had found at Mycenae. As if that were not enough, there was one last treasure—four stone axes of polished green jade and lapis lazuli. "I saw Pallas Athena in front of me," wrote Heinrich, "holding in her hands those treasures which are more valuable than all those I uncovered at Mycenae. . . . I cried for joy, fondled and kissed her feet. I thanked her from the bottom of my heart." He was later to smuggle the axes out of the country. He was not to be reformed.

Heinrich's last visit to Hissarlik uncovered more than treasure. At long last, he discovered the part of Hissarlik that matched the Bronze Age palace at Tiryns and the Bronze Age pottery he had unearthed at Mycenae. Historians are still wondering whether Schliemann fully understood what this latest find meant. What it meant, of course, is that the part of Hissarlik that he had maintained was Homeric Troy (Troy 2) did not date from the Bronze Age and was therefore *not* the Troy of Homer's *Iliad*. The books and articles that he had published were all wrong. Moreover, if this newly discovered layer of the mound (later called Troy 6) was Homer's Troy, he had thrown great heaps of it away. During his earlier attacks on Hissarlik, he had dug straight through the layer that he was trying to find. In his frenzy, he had destroyed buildings and artifacts that dated from the time of the Trojan War.

Wilhelm Dörpfeld, who excavated Troy 6 after Heinrich's death, had his own story about Heinrich's understanding of this latest find. He maintained that he broke the news to Heinrich and explained to the older man what the new findings signified: that Heinrich's earlier theories were wrong. "I discussed the matter with Schliemann, who listened carefully without saying much. He then retired into his own tent and remained incommunicado for four days. When he finally came out, he quietly said to me: 'I think you are right.'"

It was perhaps the most extraordinary moment of an extraordinary life.

In the autumn of 1890, Heinrich's earaches became agonizing. He lost nearly all of his sense of hearing. When doctors examined him, they found bony growths inside his ears. Rudolf Virchow advised Heinrich to have the growths cut out in a hospital in Germany. The operation was painful but successful. Afterward, Heinrich lay in bed reading the *Arabian Nights* (in Arabic, of course) and planning his next season's excavations.

The weeks that followed were lonely. Heinrich wrote a love letter to Sophia, praising her virtues. "At all times you were to me a loving wife, a good comrade . . . a dear companion on the road and a mother second to none." He was homesick. Against his doctor's orders, he made up his mind to leave the hospital and travel back to Athens, hoping to celebrate Christmas with his wife and children.

As he journeyed south, the pain in his ears returned and quickly grew worse. On Christmas Day 1890, he collapsed in Naples. Before a crew of doctors could agree how to treat his illness, he died.

The funeral was brilliant: Heinrich would have loved it. He was given a state burial, with a carriage drawn by eight black horses. Sophia recited Homer. Copies of *The Iliad* and *The Odyssey* were placed inside the coffin. Several hundred obituaries praised Schliemann's patience and industry, his unflagging energy, his uncanny hunches. William Gladstone, four-time prime minister of England, wrote that "Either his generosity without his energy, or his energy without his generosity might well have gained celebrity; in their union they were no less than wonderful." The inscription above the tomb read, *To the Hero Schliemann*.

Wilhelm Dörpfeld said, more simply, "Rest in peace. You have done enough."

What had he done? He had labored to prove that Homer's poetic world was true. He had done his energetic best to find Troy. Though most scholars now agree that Homeric Troy (Troy 6 or Troy 7) was located at Hissarlik, others await further proof. Today's archaeologists mourn the carelessness of Heinrich's excavations and the dishonesty that made him hedge about his finds. Heinrich Schliemann was a man who did things on a large scale, and his mistakes were not small ones.

Nevertheless, he took the world by storm. As ruthless as Achilles, as cunning as Odysseus, he rebelled against a commonplace fate. His hunger for a heroic life, his craving to *be* somebody, were not in vain. He did become rich; he did become famous; he did find lost cities and buried treasure. He spoke twenty-two languages. He wrote twelve books. Though he could not prove every detail of Homer's story, he changed the way archaeologists look at stories: he forced them to see that stories could unlock the door to great discoveries.

His excavations at Hissarlik, Mycenae, and Tiryns brought the Bronze Age to life. He once bragged: "Wherever I put my spade I always discovered new worlds for archaeology." It was true.

Many of his ideas were prophetic. Some of his most outlandish hunches—that the ancient people of Tiryns and Mycenae spoke Greek, for example—were later proved true by scholars who had the tools and training he lacked.

All his life, Heinrich was a lucky man, and he knew it. "I have had more luck than foresight in my life," he admitted. It could also be said that he made his own luck. He spared no effort and he never gave up. In the second half of his life, he had the good fortune to win the loyalty of three exceptional people: Sophia Schliemann loved and comforted him. Rudolf Virchow and Wilhelm Dörpfeld were his teachers, his counselors, and his friends.

Heinrich Schliemann wanted his life to be like a story—and it was. His rampant imagination changed archaeology forever. Some of the tales he told—like the tale of Sophia wrapping "Priam's treasure" in her red shawl—are everlasting, false though they may be. Heinrich's stories are chronic and irresistible. They are part of the Schliemann legacy. Storyteller, archaeologist, and crook—Heinrich Schliemann left his mark upon the world.

Notes and Comments

Though I have consulted all the books in the bibliography, the following sources were especially helpful:

Deuel, Leo. *Memoirs of Heinrich Schliemann: A Documentary Portrait Drawn from His Autobiographical Writings, Letters, and Excavation Reports.* Heinrich Schliemann from his own point of view. Schliemann's personality—his excitement, his conceit, his romanticism—manifests itself in every line. The editor, Leo Deuel, provides valuable background information.

Ludwig, Emil. *Schliemann: The Story of a Gold-Seeker.* Emil Ludwig was the first biographer to grapple with the great mound of writing that Schliemann left behind (two trunks full of materials written in ten different languages). When Ludwig was young, he met the aging Schliemann. After Schliemann's death, he interviewed Sophia Schliemann about her life with her husband.

Traill, David A. *Schliemann of Troy: Treasure and Deceit.* David Traill is the most skeptical of Schliemann's biographers. He has spent two decades studying Schliemann's life, working tirelessly to try to sort through Schliemann's half-truths and downright lies. Traill is a meticulous researcher and Heinrich Schliemann's sternest judge.

Moorehead, Caroline. *Lost and Found: The 9,000 Treasures of Troy: Heinrich Schliemann and the Gold That Got Away.* Caroline Moorehead's biography is also a story of the "Trojan Gold" and its disappearance during the Second World War. Though Moorehead is familiar with Traill's research, and rightly skeptical of Schliemann's stories, her view of the man himself is more tolerant than Traill's.

Wood, Michael. *In Search of the Trojan War.* Wood's book (and the accompanying videotapes) was enormously helpful in explaining the history and archaeology of Schliemann's Homeric Quest. Wood also has a knack for explaining archaeology to the layperson.

Poole, Lynn and Gray. *One Passion, Two Loves: The Story of Heinrich and Sophia Schliemann, Discoverers of Troy.* The Pooles interviewed Alex Mélas, the last living grandchild of Heinrich and Sophia Schliemann, who shared family stories with them and showed them documents that had never been published before. A good source for details about the Schliemanns' domestic life.

Chapter I
p. 3 "the mysterious and the marvelous" Deuel, p. 23.
p. 3 "Behind our garden . . ." Ibid., p. 24.
p. 4 "Father . . ." Ibid., p. 25.
p. 5 "my separation from my little bride" Ibid., p. 28.

Chapter II
p. 9 "The view of Hamburg . . ." Deuel, p. 39.
p. 9 "I would never again . . ." Ibid., p. 42.
p. 10 "flew like a seabird . . ." Ibid., p. 43.
p. 10 "I barely saved my life . . ." Ibid., p. 46.
p. 10 "gave my body over to the sharks" Ludwig, p. 24.
p. 11 "God must have chosen me . . ." Deuel, p. 51.
p. 11 "I felt reborn" Ibid., p. 52.
p. 11 "Friendships were made . . ." Ibid.
p. 12 "crowned with the fullest success" Ibid., p. 54
p. 13 "the greatest disaster" Ibid., p. 55.
p. 14 "swindling" "cunning" "immense love of money" Ibid., p. 71.
p. 14 Description of the falsified diary noted by Traill, p. 12.
p. 15 "I lay more dead than alive. . . ." Deuel, pp. 83–84.

Chapter III
p. 18 "All through the war . . ." Moorehead, p. 46.
p. 18 "How is it possible . . ." Ludwig, p. 74.
p. 18 "I cannot remain . . ." Ibid., p. 79.
p. 18 "How is it . . ." Payne, p. 77.
p. 21 "downright falsehoods . . ." Deuel, p. 127.

Chapter IV
p. 29 "the fatherland of my darling Homer" Moorehead, p. 70.
pp. 30–31 "It is very possible . . ." Traill, pp. 45–46.
p. 34 "I completely shared . . ." Deuel, p. 153.

p. 34 "The beautiful hill of Hissarlik . . ." Ibid., p. 154.
p. 35 "Frank Calvert, the famous archaeologist . . ." Traill, p. 56.
p. 35 "a braggart and bluffer" Deuel, p. vii.

Chapter V
p. 37 "because otherwise she cannot love . . ." Traill, p. 67.
p. 37 "a good and loving heart" Moorehead, p. 92.
p. 38 "Why do you wish . . ." "Because my parents . . ." Ludwig,
    pp. 114–115.
p. 39 "friend for life" "dearest husband" "adored wife . . ." Poole,
    p. 129.
p. 39 "I knew I loved . . ." Moorehead, p. 99.
p. 41 "Troy . . . was sacked twice . . ." Kennedy, pp. 94–95.
p. 43 "It was an entirely new world . . ." Deuel, p. 220.
p. 49 "The treasure was packed . . ." Ibid., p. 207.
p. 49 "the greatest and most important . . ." Ibid., p. 197.

Chapter VI
p. 54 "I kept everything valuable . . ." Deuel, p. 213.
p. 55 "in the name of humanity" Moorehead, p. 141.
p. 58 "I have found . . ." Ibid., pp. 167–168.
p. 59 "I have gazed . . ." Wood, p. 68.
p. 60 "All right, let's call him Schultze!" Moorehead, p. 170.
p. 62 "Schliemann's greatest discovery" Deuel, p. 287.
p. 63 "Palace of Troy" [Schliemann named his palace Ilíou
    Mélathron, which can be translated as either "Palace" or
    "Hut" of Ilium (or Troy).] Ibid., p. 281.
p. 63 "but it contained . . ." Ibid., p. 347.
pp. 64–65 "Throughout my own girlhood . . ." Ibid.
p. 65 "Once again the gods granted me . . ." Ibid., pp. 314–315.

Chapter VII
p. 68 "I saw Pallas Athena . . ." Deuel, p. 344.
p. 69 "I discussed the matter . . ." Moorehead, p. 235.
pp. 69–70 "At all times . . ." Ibid., p. 229.
p. 70 "Either his generosity . . ." Deuel, p. 352.
p. 70 "Rest in peace . . ." Traill, p. 297.
p. 71 "Wherever I put my spade . . ." Moorehead, pp. 212–213.
p. 72 "I have had more luck . . ." Deuel, p. 8.

Bibliography

Bahn, Paul G., editor. *Cambridge Illustrated History of Archaeology.* Cambridge: Cambridge University Press, 1996.

Braymer, Marjorie. *The Walls of Windy Troy: A Biography of Heinrich Schliemann.* New York: Harcourt, Brace, 1960.

Caselli, Giovanni. *In Search of Troy: One Man's Quest for Homer's Fabled City.* New York: Peter Bedrick, 1999.

Ceram, C. W. *Gods, Graves, & Scholars: The Story of Archaeology.* 2nd rev. ed. New York: Vintage, 1986.

Deuel, Leo. *Memoirs of Heinrich Schliemann: A Documentary Portrait Drawn from His Autobiographical Writings, Letters, and Excavation Reports.* London: Hutchinson, 1978.

Duchêne, Hervé. *Golden Treasures of Troy: The Dream of Heinrich Schliemann.* Discoveries series. New York: Abrams, 1996.

Homer. *The Iliad.* Translated by Richmond Lattimore. Chicago: University of Chicago Press, 1961.

Homer. *The Odyssey.* Translated by Robert Fagles. New York: Viking, 1996.

Kennedy, Maev. *The History of Archaeology.* Surrey, England: Quadrillion/Octopus, 1998.

Ludwig, Emil. *Schliemann: The Story of a Gold-Seeker.* Boston: Little, Brown, 1931.

Mohen, Jean-Pierre, and Christiane Eluère. *The Bronze Age in Europe.* Discoveries series. New York: Abrams, 2000.

Moorehead, Caroline. *Lost and Found: The 9,000 Treasures of Troy: Heinrich Schliemann and the Gold That Got Away.* New York: Viking, 1994.

Payne, Robert. *The Gold of Troy: The Story of Heinrich Schliemann and the Buried Cities of Ancient Greece.* New York: Funk & Wagnalls, 1959.

Poole, Lynn and Gray. *One Passion, Two Loves: The Story of Heinrich and Sophia Schliemann, Discoverers of Troy.* New York: Crowell, 1966.

Traill, David A. *Schliemann of Troy: Treasure and Deceit.* New York: St. Martin's, 1995.

Tyler, Deborah. *The Greeks and Troy.* New York: Dillon, 1993.

Ventura, Piero, and Gian Paolo Ceserani. *In Search of Troy.* Morristown, N.J.: Silver Burdett, 1985.

Wood, Michael. *In Search of the Trojan War.* New York: Facts on File, 1985.

BILL EASUM

BILL TENNY-BRITTIAN

UNDER THE RADAR

LEARNING FROM RISK-TAKING CHURCHES

ABINGDON PRESS / Nashville

UNDER THE RADAR
LEARNING FROM RISK-TAKING CHURCHES

Copyright © 2005 by Abingdon Press

All rights reserved.

This book is printed on acid-free paper.

Library of Congress Cataloging-in-Publication Data
Easum, William M., 1939-
    Under the radar : learning from risk-taking churches / Bill Easum and Bill Tenny-Brittian.
        p. cm.
    ISBN 0-687-49373-0 (binding: adhesive : alk. paper)
    1. Church. 2. Church renewal—North America. 3. Church growth—North America. I. Tenny-Brittian, William. II. Title.

BV600.3.E28 2005
277.3′083—dc22

                                                                    2005008028

All scripture quotations are taken from the *New Revised Standard Version of the Bible,* copyright 1989, Division of Christian Education of the National Council of the Churches of Christ in the United States of America. Used by permission. All rights reserved.

05 06 07 08 09 10 11 12 13 14—10 9 8 7 6 5 4 3 2 1

MANUFACTURED IN THE UNITED STATES OF AMERICA

CONTENTS

114397

PREFACE

The Ancient-Present Church

During the last ten years it has become increasingly apparent to those who read the signs of the times that a huge crack has opened up between established congregations and those presently emerging all over North America.[1] This crack is so huge that it is re-creating the religious landscape of North America. Twenty years from now, more than likely, it will be difficult to recognize North American Christianity.

North America is going backward in time—back to a time in the far distant past. Back, way back, to the supernatural, mystical, polytheistic world that gave birth to Christianity—back to the first few centuries A.D. As a result, a form of Christianity is emerging that has not been seen since Constantine legitimatized the church and the ensuing councils completed the task of institutionalizing and domesticating Christianity. Whereas the Reformation signaled the birth of a new way of doing Christianity, this present crack is signaling the failure of institutional Christianity as we know it and the birth of a new breed of congregation. Many of these new churches are under most people's radar.

Most church members find it is impossible to give any credibility to this new breed of church. Either they can't count it, it's just another fad that will soon pass, or it scares them to death because they sense that it might be the real deal. Still, this emerging movement is as vibrant and authentic as the day Peter hung

v

upside-down on a cross or Ignatius pleaded with the church at Rome not to get in the way of the Romans feeding him to the lions.

We have been tracking the emerging church's journey now for a decade. It's an *ancient-present* form of Christianity that has never been experienced by any group of Christians in North America. All of us need to pay attention and learn from it. This book examines several expressions of these under-the-radar congregations.

Bill Easum
Bill Tenny-Brittian

INTRODUCTION

Who Will Benefit from Reading *Under the Radar*?

Recently, we began to research a group of churches that defy most of the traditional wisdom of our time. You hold the results of that research in your hand. Our intention is to introduce you to some of these churches in hopes that it might open some eyes to the multitude of opportunities for witnessing to the good news that are opening up at the beginning of this millennium. We trust you will be open enough to hear the still small voice speaking. If you're tired of the "normal" church, read on.

Misunderstanding of the Meaning of "Church"

In order to get the most out of this book we need to consider how off base most people are when we think of the word *church*. If we're honest, most of us think of a building when we hear the word *church*. We say "I'm going to church," or we invite people to "come to my church." Our usage of the word betrays our misunderstanding of the word. For most church leaders, the marks of a *real* church include:

- a building
- an ordained pastor (so they can speak orthodoxy for the church)
- a weekly worship service and other "church" programs

- "church" polity (whether board-, deacon-, or elder-controlled)
- enough members to financially support all of the above

The fallacy of our use of the word *church* is hard to miss when we realize that it wasn't until about 323 that the first known church building popped up. Until that time, most churches gathered in homes, catacombs, dungeons, street corners, and even "upper rooms." So, put it out of your mind that place or space has anything whatsoever to do with church. Neither is the church a policy-making group, a place where our batteries are charged, or our personal possession.

So, what is "church"? Jesus gave us the definition of *church*: "For where two or three are gathered in my name, I am there among them" (Matthew 18:20).

The church is a movement of God's people. But that's not all. In Jesus' day, the word *ecclesia* meant a gathering or assembly of people who *came together to accomplish a task*. Therefore, a church is a God-movement with the sole purpose of bringing the world to Jesus Christ.

How many "churches" could survive this definition of *church*?

Now with this definition in mind, we are ready to examine some churches that are under the radar setting the stage for the next wave of spiritual explosions in this land. I am only going to preview a couple of these churches so you can see the diversity of what is emerging.

Alpha Church (www.alphachurch.org)

Alpha Church is the first and currently the only one of its kind: a full-service cyberchurch. Yes, you read that right. Alpha Church accomplishes *everything* that the typical church can accomplish including communion, baptisms, offerings, sermons, singing, and so on, but it does so on the Internet.

You can just hear the naysayers: "That's not a church!" But so far more than six thousand regular participants and more than one hundred members in the Alpha Church say you're wrong; it is a community of Christians gathering to spread the gospel, and it doesn't exist in a place.

The pastor, Patricia E. Walker, suggests that in the future her site will include holographic opportunities. In my (BE) book *Growing Spiritual Redwoods*, I wrote about the mythical "Church of the Virtual Resurrection" in which I imaged what a holographic worship service might look like. The future is almost here, and it is changing our concept of "church."

Alpha Church is certainly not the first cyber community on the Web. The first cyberchurch that got national press was www.zchurch.com. However, communities like www.easumbandy.com and www.theooze.com are gaining popularity as online communities as well. But Alpha Church is the first *full-service* online community. The cyberchurch community has just begun.

Imago Dei Community
(www.imagodeicommunity.com)

Imago Dei Community in Portland, Oregon, isn't the kind of church where you would expect to find more than 500 twenty-somethings worshiping together. Stepping into their worship space is like stepping into another century. There is clearly a narthex and a nave, the ceiling architectural beams look like you've walked into an upside-down sailing ship with all the futtocks and ribs exposed. People sit in old polished pews to worship.

Ancient-future doesn't quite describe Imago Dei. When the worship starts, the band cranks out urban grunge tunes indigenous to the Pacific Northwest. The words to the tunes are projected on the wall—poorly, because the walls weren't designed for presentations. There are a few candles, but with the exception of the building's architecture, there's nothing gothic about what's going on here—not so much as a chant in the house.

So, what's remarkable enough about Imago Dei that it should warrant your attention? Their seamless wedding of arts in culture and monasticism, a marriage we call Renaissance, Arts, and Monasticism. What makes Imago Dei unique is the way they have woven the arts and artists into the DNA of their community. Whereas, in most churches, the addition of the arts is something added on to enhance the program, Imago Dei has embedded art into the life and culture of the congregation. Art isn't an add-on, it's who they are.

Art is so embedded into their culture that Imago Dei helped establish the Artistery (pronounced ART-is-ter-ee, like *monastery*). The Artistery is a monasticlike community for artists who desire to learn the spiritual and artistic disciplines of practicing and refining their art in a Christian environment. The Artistery is a one-year home to five young men who live in a single residence in the Brooklyn arts community in Portland. These artists are required to work at a job outside of the Artistery and to provide a portion of the living expenses. They also share community chores such as cooking, cleaning, and providing simple maintenance. Their monastic-artistic duties include a weekly spiritual group study meeting, attendance at church, and attendance at the monthly Imago Dei potluck fellowship dinner. They must also provide a weekly class in their artistic specialty, begin and complete a new artistic project each month, and produce a show of their work sometime during their stay. Art from the Artisterians can regularly be viewed on the Imago Dei Community Web site.

Upper Room Churches

The house church movement has been gaining momentum in the United States over the last decade. Two kinds of house churches seem to exist at the moment: organic and networked. Neil Cole's organic House Church Movement, www.cmaresources.com, has over seventy-five house churches based on his life transformation group (LTG) model of discipleship. These house churches are each independent, although most began using the LTG model. There is little or no accountability exercised over the leaders; however, because of the organic DNA that is imbued upon them through Cole's initial training, most of them multiply rapidly and are receiving an abundant harvest in their communities.

The Rock Christian Church in Seattle is an example of a networked house church (www.therockcc.us). Bill Tenny-Brittian is the lead pastor for the network. This networked house church is held accountable by the pastor and an advisory board, and the network is a part of a mainline denomination. To maintain accountability and the DNA, each house church leader is a part of an accountability group; they receive regular training; they have access to materials and programs custom-written for the house church experience. In addition, each house church is expected to raise up leaders to begin new house churches at least annually.

It is our opinion that the postmodern will gravitate to house churches based on their anti-institutional stance.

So What's the Buzz?

We've given you three examples of churches that most people don't know much about that I believe have the potential to help chart the course over the next few decades. Since none of them are proven commodities, we could be wrong. However, by the time they do appear on the radar screen, we believe they will be part of a major trend of the near future. So, what can we learn from them?

The day of cloning is coming to an end. Many church leaders are still trying to clone great churches like Saddleback and Willow Creek. It might be working for some at the moment, but probably not for long. Instead, find God's model for your environment. Contextual ministry is the mark of every successful and faithful church in America.

Get to know your niche. Nothing takes the place of knowing the heartbursts of your neighbors, the hearbeat of the culture, and the sounds of the community. Before you plant or start new ministries, get in touch with the spiritual life of the unchurched, dechurched, and the never-churched folks around you.

Don't allow yourself to be boxed in by the trappings of the traditional church. If they aren't working now—and they aren't—they won't be working in the near future.

The future is open to those who can dream and conceive of new things because we live in a time when God is doing a new thing. We hope you can see it.

CHAPTER ONE

WHAT IS CHURCH?

I (BTB) was sitting in a coffee shop in Seattle enjoying my grande, nonfat, no foam, single-ristretto, sugar-free hazelnut latte. (Hey, this is a book on the emerging church, and I'm in Seattle, right?) A half-dozen customers were there that morning, so I decided to ask them to describe their understanding of the word *church*.

Now, keep in mind that the church culture in the Seattle Metro complex is considered by many to be the most unchurched region in the United States. Only 7 percent of the population show up in church more than once a month and recent figures suggest that about 64 percent are officially "unaffiliated," which means when we're asked, we claim we're not a part of *any* religion. So, when I started asking people "What is the church?" I was ready for all sorts of answers.

What they said, though, surprised me. Rachel, age 23, defined it as "a place for gathering and worship." This was the answer I generally expected. It's also the answer most people tend to give because over the past seventeen hundred years or so the worship center has been synonymous with the word *church*. Scott, also 23, offered a more spiritually focused answer. He said the church is "a spiritual place within yourself for worship and security." This was the kind of answer I expected from the Seattle crowd: a response focused on individuality and independence. And then came a surprising answer. Ellen, age 46, said that the church was "a people who support each other with a common belief." Add the word *Christian* to her definition, and we could be on our way

1

to a biblical definition. Except for one problem. Although most people who have been active in the Christian church for any period of time might agree with Ellen's definition, her comment is incomplete and not a reflection of how most church members define *church*.

Misunderstandings of the Word *Church*

You don't have to talk to church members very long to discover that a variety of misunderstandings about the meaning of the word *church* exist. Here are a few of the most used descriptions of the church in our everyday conversations.

The Church Is a Place to Go

The most common misunderstanding of the church is that it is a place where people go to do something. Almost every Christian has talked about "going to church." When most people think of the church, they think of a building in which something happens: worship, Christian education, small group fellowships, choir practice, board meetings, committee meetings, subcommittee meetings, staff meetings, deacon meetings—well you get the picture.

However, before Constantine's proclamation in A.D. 313, there were virtually no church buildings. According to the Scriptures, people met in houses, though for a time they showed up at the temple or in the synagogues, but that was pretty short-lived. There are some who have suggested that Paul rented a community building for worship,[1] but as the Roman persecution of Christians increased, any sort of Christian gathering was outlawed, and it became too risky to set aside a building for a church. Thus, for more than two hundred years the church had no physical location. And we might also add that the Christian movement did quite well during that time.

But after Constantine pronounced Christianity as the state religion, the cathedrals, church buildings, and chapels began to emerge throughout the empire and the image and understanding of *church* began to change as the years went by. Seventeen hundred years later, when we hear the word *church*, we immediately visualize a building with a steeple where we go to practice our Christianity.

2

The Church Is a Place Where Our Batteries Are Charged

A lot of people speak of going to church in the same way they talk about going to a store to buy something. For many, the church is where we go to get our weekly dose of religion and morality. They have no concept that church is not where you get something but where you give praise to God. People go to church to receive religious education, except there isn't any homework to expand their knowledge beyond class, no tests to keep them focused, and no grades to indicate their progress. People go there to get "spiritual food" as if the church was a restaurant; however, they may leave "the church" if they don't get fed, as if the church was supposed to spoon-feed them as well. And of course, people go there in the hope that their children will get a healthy dose of morality—almost as if they hope that "the church" can civilize their little ankle-biters.

The Church Is a Policy-Making Group

A third common meaning for the word *church* is as a policy-making group. This is most evident when someone complains about a decision at their church: "I wish the church would leave the music alone. I just don't like their decisions." In this case, the "church" is probably just the worship committee, but since everyone seems to be going along with the changes, that is, everyone is singing at church, then it must be the church who made the decision. Many established Christians think of "church ownership" being the right to sit on committees and make decisions.

The Church Is My Personal Possession!

A fourth misunderstanding of the church is that it is "our" personal possession populated by "our" friends. We tend to experience this anytime we visit a church outside of our tradition or when we visit a church where we don't know anybody. In these cases we're very sure that "this wasn't my church," because *my church* is made up of my friends, relatives, and all those familiar faces—even if I don't know their names—that I've come to know over the years.

Each of these misunderstandings contains a shadow of truth. But if we wrap up all these parts into one, we still don't get the fullness, or rather the simplicity, of what the Scriptures teach about church.

A Definition Is More Than Semantics

Before we get to a biblical definition of the church, we need to answer one question: Why does a definition of the word *church* matter so much? After all, isn't it all just a matter of semantics? We've been calling the church building the "church" and saying "going to church" when we mean we're attending a worship service for so long, what does it really matter?

We think it matters a great deal. The word *church* has been so diluted by popular usage that it is pretty well useless in trying to describe what the Bible and the early church were talking about. As a result, much of what churches do has little to do with the function of the church as described in the Scriptures.

It would be handy if we could inject a new word into our vocabulary that carries with it the true meaning of church, but that probably isn't going to happen anytime soon. So it is important that we deconstruct what the word *church* has come to mean, at least in the church's understanding, so we are all on the same page.

But the real reason we need to redefine *church* is because its common usage is killing Christianity in the United States.[2] Not only does it color how Christians conceive of what a normal "church" looks like, but we believe it is also one of the reasons fewer people on a spiritual journey today participate in a church—the common understanding of the word has prejudiced them against it.

In the past, the church was the most effective way to reach new people for Jesus Christ. Not anymore. In a recent Gallup poll, 90 percent of the American population believe in God, but where do they go to explore their thoughts on God?[3] Anywhere *but* the church. At best, polls indicate less than 35 percent of Americans go to church with any regularity, and even that number is suspect. The fact is, people are interested in spirituality, but not in the church. One of the reasons is the present misunderstandings about what it means to be a church.

4

And yet consistently we find that the most effective way to introduce unchurched, irreligious people to Jesus Christ is to start new churches. This may well seem counterintuitive, but it is no less true. So for the past twenty years or so, mainline denominations,[4] as well as many other denominations, have been throwing a lot of money the way of starting new churches. To start a church, the denominational leaders hire an ordained pastor to go into an area where the demographics show significant growth—typically in fast-growing suburbs. The denomination then buys about five acres for the future church. Next the pastor is given a fairly large sum of money to do marketing. Sometimes the pastor gathers a team from other denominational churches to do telemarketing. Sometimes they do a direct mail campaign. Occasionally they even produce commercials. When a core group of members is gathered for the fledgling congregation, the denomination often constructs a building on the property and the church has a grand opening.

This worked pretty well for a decade or two, and many churches were started across the United States. However, it was fairly expensive to start new churches that way—often as much as $2 million considering the costs of land, new construction, the pastor's salary, marketing, and programming for the first couple of years. By the time the 1960s arrived, this method of church planting generally produced congregations of less than three hundred people and more often congregations of just over one hundred. With the decline in church attendance across the nation, and the corresponding drop in offerings, denominations can't afford to keep up the pace of starting these kinds of church plants, so they have continually cut back on the number of new church starts.

Today it's a rare denomination that has an extra one or two million in the bank for starting a new church that will only net a congregation of three hundred, let alone one hundred. So they've been scrambling, trying to find new ways to start churches. But most of the denominations are stuck in the old definition of *church*. To most church leaders, the word *church* means that a church has to:

- have a building for the church
- have an ordained pastor (so they can speak orthodoxy for the church)

- have a worship service and other programs like the church
- be organized like the church
- have enough members to financially support all of the above

Denominations can't afford to start new churches the old way, and we haven't found a new way to effectively start churches as defined by the old definitions.

Where did we go wrong? If starting new churches is the most effective way to reach the unchurched, irreligious people in our nation, what can we do? We believe the answer to this question is found in how we define the word *church*.

Discovering the Old Definition for a New Church

Our intention is not to offer an exhaustive, scholarly definition of the word *church*. Our intention is to provide as simple and as biblical a definition as possible in order to pave the way for an honest and open evaluation of some of the emerging church expressions that often defy the common use of the word *church*.

For better or worse, the word *church* is with us to stay. The English word itself went through an evolution that can be traced back to *cirice* in Old English, to *kirika* in Germanic usage and, according to most scholars, ultimately to the more modern Greek word *kyriakon*, which means the Lord's house.[5] However, others think the evolution more likely developed from the Latin word *circulus*, meaning circle, a word that was known in all the Celtic dialects long before the Greek word *kyriakon* was developed.[6]

The problem with either of these etymologies is that *none* of these words in any way relate to the word or the concept Jesus and the apostles used to describe what we have come to know as the church. The word they used was *ecclesia*. Jesus did not say to Peter, "On this rock I will build *the Lord's house*" in Matthew 16:18. Instead he said, "On this rock I will build my church" *(ecclesia)*, which doesn't sound anything like the word *church* as it is used today. *Ecclesia* is the word used nearly every time we read "church" in the Bible. The question we need to ask is, why did Jesus and the apostles choose this word to describe what we have come to know as church?

In Jesus' day, the word *ecclesia* meant a gathering or assembly of people. Sounds like a terrific description of the church today: people getting together. We do that pretty well in the church. But the word has a bit more of a focused connotation. For one, the word literally means "the called-out ones." This implies that the people assembled were called together for some specific purpose

A review of the word in writings outside of the Bible finds that *ecclesia* almost always describes an assembly of people who come together to accomplish some task, whether that means working, voting, debating, or making decisions. There are few, if any, cases where the word is used to denote getting together for the sake of getting together.

Now I can hear my own mind crying, "Foul! We get together for worship and *that's* a purpose." And the rational side of the brain jumps in and agrees. But wait, there's more to *ecclesia* than a rousing worship service.

In the Septuagint, the Greek translation of the Old Testament, the word *ecclesia* can be found about seventy times. In almost all of those times the word is used to designate an assembly that's been called together for a specific purpose beyond a regularly scheduled worship service. These gatherings were often to behold the Lord's mighty works or to hear the commands of the Lord such as in Numbers 20:8[7] and Deuteronomy 4:10-11.[8]

Jesus, however, is the author of the definition of what the church is. Although he only used the word twice in the Gospels, he apparently communicated to his disciples what he was getting at when he referred to the church. In the first place he said, "I will build my church" (Matthew 16:18). Then in Matthew 18 he teaches his disciples how to handle sin in the church. He concludes his discourse in verse 20 with what can only be described as his definition of the church. Jesus said, "For where two or three are gathered in my name, I am there among them" (Matthew 18:20).

7

Jesus gave us the definition of church: "For where two or three are gathered in my name, I am there among them"
(Matthew 18:20).

Our mind intercedes once again. "See, that's what I said. Whenever we get together, that's when we're the church." And our rational brain, which is used to putting pieces of puzzles together and so has learned a little something so far, says, "Just getting together isn't what *ecclesia* is all about; it's about gathering for a *purpose*." That means being intentional about why we're getting together—and the church is the *ecclesia* when it's gathered together "in my name" to do the Lord's work and to accomplish the Lord's will.

Now, lest we wonder what the Lord's will is, it can pretty well be summed up in what we call the *Four Greats*, each of which were spoken by our Lord:

- The First Great Commandment: Love the Lord with everything you've got.
- The Second Great Commandment: Love others like Jesus loved us.
- The Great Invitation: Follow me—don't just ask "What would Jesus do?" *Do what Jesus did.*
- The Great Commission: Make more disciples.

The church is any companionship of disciples gathered to intentionally follow Jesus and accomplish the Four Greats.

Using our Lord's definition of the church, the word has nothing to do with:

- A specified place
- An organized worship service
- Anything institutional
- Anyone ordained for anything

8

Before Constantine, Christians met in their travels, drew the sign of the fish, recognized their common faith, and began to share together their lives and faith in Jesus, or as Paul says, to participate in the body of Christ. Bingo—they became the church. Perhaps that's why Christians were first referred to as people of "the Way."[9] Unlike so many other religions, including Judaism, Christianity had nothing to do with a place but with a Christian's relationship to Christ. What made a gathering of people "the church" was when two or three came together because of their affinity for Jesus and his mission. Therefore the essence of "church" has nothing to do with place or space or even an organized service of worship. The essence of the church is relationships forged around the risen Christ for the purpose of spreading the good news.

Church. It's one of the most misused and abused words in the English language. Its misuse has been hurting the cause of Christ for years, and yet it was his church for which Jesus was willing to die. It's time we redefine the church to match what Jesus and his disciples meant. For the sake of this book, and as an invitation to all, we'd like to offer this definition: *Any companionship of disciples gathered to intentionally follow Jesus and accomplish the Four Greats.*

Most of this book is dedicated to those men and women who have taken the Four Greats seriously and have been called out to start new and innovative expressions of the church. Some don't have a building to meet in—and never plan to. Some will never be larger than maybe twenty people—on purpose. Others don't make a living doing their church planting—and don't intend to. If we use the definition of church most of us have been raised with, virtually none of these qualify as a church. But thankfully, Jesus' definition of the church is the only one that counts, so the examples of churches that follow is among the list of the faithful.

What to Expect

Each of the churches we've chosen represent, in broad categories, a variety of different models that have been effective in their contexts. Some of the churches are very small, especially by typical American church growth standards. Others, such as Alpha Church, have more than six thousand participants each week. Most of the pastors of these churches expressed concern over being a part of this book because they understand the temptation by some to clone models. Our hope is that these churches will be inspirational in imagining and creating new congregations designed for their own unique contexts.

But before you jump in to look at these "new" models of the American emerging church movement, take time to *carefully* read chapter 2, "Attack of the Clones." We promise, it will save you a lot of grief later.

Take Two

- Take a few minutes some morning to ask the locals at your coffee shop what words come to mind when they hear the word *church*. However, be careful to simply listen and not to get defensive. The answers will likely disturb you, but it will be an enlightening experience.
- Would you agree that the word *church* has been so misused that most people don't have a clue as to its real meaning?
- Which one of the misunderstandings of the word *church* do you hear most often? How do you respond to them? Or do you? If not, why?
- How do you feel about our definition of the word *church*? Can you see how it might open up new forms of church?

CHAPTER TWO

ATTACK OF THE CLONES

Both of us are more Trekkies than *Star Wars* junkies, but the *Star Wars* movie *Attack of the Clones* struck us as a fitting title for this chapter. For whatever reasons, it seems that whenever a congregation is blessed by God and reaches thousands of people for Jesus Christ, well-meaning church leaders study it and try to clone it within their own contexts. No matter how often a Rick Warren or Bill Hybels tells us that it isn't possible to duplicate their churches, too many of us still try. We buy their books, listen to their tapes, and go to their seminars only to become disheartened when the transplant doesn't work back home. The problem is, just like the scientists' ongoing attempts to clone sheep, goats, and guinea pigs, cloning churches is an imperfect process that more often than not leads to a premature demise.

Scientists are struggling to discover the answer to why clones are weak, malformed, and short-lived. Those who have studied the church in the United States have long been struggling with the same question. Why is it that when we try to start another Willow Creek, or when we try to reform an existing congregation into a Saddleback, we most often end up with a weak, malformed, and short-lived church? Although the reasons are probably more complicated than we can imagine, we offer the following three causes.

- We're not Bill Hybels. Dolly the sheep may have been cloned, but the heroes of the twenty-first-century American church will not be clones of today's church heroes. What

11

makes Bill Hybels and other great church leaders outstanding is the way in which God has gifted them and how they've dealt with all the curves life has thrown them. They are effective leaders of their congregations because they are who they are and they did "their thing." Every successful church model is developed by a leader who understands who they are and what works for them.

- Transplanting a church model is a bit like trying to transplant a kidney. Unless a transplant is between identical twins, the donors and recipients are immunologically incompatible, that is, the body will naturally try to reject the kidney because it's "foreign." The same thing happens whenever someone tries to plant a Willow Creek outside of South Barrington. What works there won't work elsewhere because the context is different.

- So far, cloning animals has been an imperfect process at best. Whenever scientists try to clone an animal, they have to deal with genetic mutations caused from impurities within the host egg. To date, there have been no perfect clones.

Just as there's no such thing as a perfect clone, there are no perfectly cloned churches either. No matter how hard we try, we end up with a distorted copy of the original.

In these cloned churches, the focus is on "being like" the model rather than on being indigenous to the context. This emphasis of striving to be like another church is to cease seeking to be faithful in the local community context.

Throw Out the Clone, but Keep the Bathwater

To clone or not to clone isn't much of a question. There's only one Willow Creek and there's only one Saddleback. What worked for these two churches was their commitment to reach the people in their community in ways that were effective in their specific locale.

On the other hand, there is much to be learned from these churches that we can use if we're interested in becoming an authentic church that takes the Four Greats seriously.

Adopt and Adapt

The first thing to remember when you're tempted to clone a great idea is to remember that there are very few new and original great ideas. Most great ideas bubble up to reality because somebody saw a need in their context and figured out how to meet the need by adapting or adopting something they'd seen or heard about somewhere else. For instance, I (BTB) visit the Renaissance Café almost every Sunday morning for breakfast because they have some of the best scrambled eggs in the community. The eggs are cooked to perfection every single time, and they are the lightest, fluffiest eggs I've ever had. What makes them so special is that the cook doesn't fry the eggs, he cooks them using the ultrahot steam from the milk-frothing wand of a full-size commercial espresso machine. If you've ever frothed milk, you know that the steam wand injects super heated steam into the milk. This stirs it and froths it. If you've ever whipped eggs, you may have noticed how much they froth up. It wasn't a huge leap for the cook to make a connection—and he discovered the side benefit that the eggs not only whipped and frothed when he used the steam wand, they cooked to perfection as well. So now he has the best eggs in town because he was able to adopt and adapt.

Christian leadership has got to learn to do the same thing. It's not about cloning but about seeing what's exciting and adaptable from these under-the-radar churches and then adopting and tweaking those key strategies that may work in our particular context.

Contextualize

Willow Creek, Saddleback, and each of the church expressions underscored in this book have much to teach us about faithful contextualization of ministry. By looking to see how each has evaluated their settings and adapted their ministries to fit, we can explore the possibilities of what might work in our own backyards.

Contextual Ministry Is the Only Way to Be Faithful

Contextual ministry is the mark of every successful and faithful church in America. It's also the mark of the under-the-radar emerging churches in America today. Not that contextual ministry for the church is anything new. It's as old as the first church in the Bible.

Pentecost is the birthday of the church. On that glorious day, the visitation of the Holy Spirit on the apostles spewed them into the street proclaiming the gospel in twelve different languages. This miracle seemed to be the end of the Tower of Babel curse, but it was not to be. There wasn't suddenly just a single language, which would mark Babel's reversal; rather, the gospel was proclaimed in the language of the people. They were able to hear the gospel in their *own* tongue—a key to contextual ministry.

Now, it took time for the apostles to get on board with what God was trying to do. The gospel was preached in Samaria and many believed. But the Jerusalem church didn't, so they sent Peter and John to check it out.[1] The gospel was preached to the Gentiles and the Holy Spirit manifested upon the new converts. But the Jerusalem church was skeptical, so they interrogated Peter who witnessed the event. The gospel was taken to Asia and to Europe, but the Jerusalem church wanted to impose its practices upon it. Paul, however, "got it." He understood that Pentecost was about context—ministry in the language, the style, and even the metaphors of the community. And so the church grew even to the ends of the earth.

But in each successive generation, the church has tried to limit the contextualization of the gospel. I (BTB) remember so vividly the reaction of an elder in my church when, as a youth, I made the "mistake" of singing George Harrison's "My Sweet Lord" at a youth retreat. Never mind that I was singing to my sweet Lord Jesus. Never mind that it was one of the first times my youth group and I were actually worshiping together. The elder was incensed that I would sing a song that wasn't in the hymnal. It wasn't worshipful to him, therefore it couldn't be worship for others, regardless of their generational status. The problem was that he wanted to impose his version of the Christian faith on a different context, the context of a different generation.

Many books have been written over the past few decades on contextualizing the gospel, so hopefully this isn't something new for you.[2] However, as you read the rest of this book and learn how other churches have chosen to engage their cultures, there are certain principles of contextualization that these church leaders have used that are important to consider—especially if you are interested in starting or sponsoring an under-the-radar emerging church.

Discovering Contexts

Before you set out to plant a new church, you will need to know more than the technicalities of how to start churches. For one, you need to know the context in which you are going to plant. Who lives there? How do they think? What is important to them? What generations are there? What kind of music do they sing? What kind of communication style connects? And so on.

But before all that, it's more important to know what kind of context *you* carry. Contrary to magnetism and marriage, when it comes to the church, likes attract. At least in the beginning, the people who commit to a congregation will look, act, and think a lot like the person who recruited them. In most cases this will be the pastor, or whoever is the evangelist for the fledgling congregation. This is critical because one of the primary reasons new churches fail is because the wrong pastor is in the right place and vice versa. There's not a lot of sense in sending a country mouse to reach city mice or the other way around. The same goes for sending a baby boomer to reach Generation Xers. It's even becoming questionable whether or not it's effective to send a suburbanite into an urban context to start church work because the values, expectations, and expressions are so different. The key to a successful ministry anywhere, whether it's in the rain forests of Brazil or a county seat in Missouri, is to match the gospel presentation to the context.

Context Is More Than Demographics

It used to be that one of the first tasks of church planting was reviewing demographics to find the most fertile neighborhood in which to plant a church. Although demographics are important in discovering population shifts, psychographics are significantly more helpful when it comes to matching planter to field. Psychographics help reveal a local population's propensity for the gospel. Psychographics disclose what is on their minds—are they concerned about their 401(k)s or about putting food on the table? Indeed, with the right psychographics package, you can even find out whether the neighbors are likely to be reading *USA Today* or if they prefer *The National Enquirer*.[3]

Get to Know Your Neighborhood

Every church has neighbors. Whether a new church chooses to own a building, rent or borrow space, or meet in homes, it will be located in both time and space. Even if it rotates its meeting place, the church has a geographic center. A windshield tour of the neighborhood has long been counted on to reveal the psychographics of the people living and working there.

For instance, if the neighborhood has a plethora of parks and play equipment and the homes have tricycles and bicycles scattered about, the neighborhood is probably a haven for families. If all the cars in the driveways are minivans, SUVs, and Volvos, the families probably come from the middle- to upper-middle-class socioeconomic group. Discerning these psychographics can seem like child's play.

However, if the neighborhood has thirty-seven-floor apartment buildings that tower over urban streets hosting second-hand clothing shops; Tai, Vietnamese, and pizza restaurants; coffee shops; a couple of bars; bus stops every other block, and a college campus, the neighborhood will obviously have some different dynamics than the one above. In fact, this neighborhood could be much more ready for a new church plant than the suburban setting, but planting a church here will be a very different enterprise. Windshield tours are helpful only in painting a broad picture of the people who live in the neighborhood. Depending on these observations to disclose much about the residents is foolhardy in most settings, and it should be considered completely unreliable in urban contexts.

Get to Know Your Neighbors

The best way to discover the potential for a new church in any setting is to get to know the neighbors. This phase of information gathering can be rather time intensive; however, if the church planter is the one doing the work, they will undoubtedly make acquaintances with a number of folks who are ready for the gospel and a church family.

There are many different ways to meet the neighbors, but some are more common than others. In Seattle, hanging out at the local coffee shops is effective. On the other hand, I (BE) found that to meet my neighbors at one church I had to shear sheep, at another play shuffle board, and at another hang out at an upscale watering hole. In the suburbs, getting involved with the PTA, Little League, or the Homeowners Association are other options.

Casey Cerretani, a church planter on First Hill, an urban neighborhood in Seattle, got to know his neighbors by visiting the local shops and restaurants to get to know the owners, managers, and clerks. From these visits, he met Dan Piecora who owns Piecora's Pizza, a favorite haunt for students and residents alike. The acquaintance blossomed and Piecora's Pizza became the initial host for the Seattle Urban Foursquare Church (where Sunday worship would end with bowls of Italian salad and huge slices of Piecora's famous pizza). Meeting the neighbors can be effective on multiple levels.

However, there's more to getting to know the neighbors than just a nod or a handshake. Learning who the neighbors are takes both active and passive listening. When I (BTB) first started hanging out at my local coffee shop, I didn't know anyone. So I would quietly sip my latte, peruse a book, and passively listen to the conversations going on around me. I learned that kids were a real focus for the families, that a lot of moms didn't work outside the home, and that most people in the neighborhood were more concerned with going on vacation or buying a boat than worrying about their stock portfolio (a serious concern for people who live less than half-a-mile north of my neighborhood). However, in time, passive listening turned into conversation.

One of the most effective ways to meet and engage your neighbors, I've learned, is to practice prayer walking. Prayer walking is taking a stroll through a neighborhood and praying for each home and business as you pass. Those who practice prayer walking testify to its effectiveness, especially in terms of meeting and affecting the neighbors. It is during frequent prayer walks that Felicity Dale, a church planter in Texas, has met those who would host home churches throughout Austin.[4] In most cases, those who practice prayer walking strike up conversations with neighbors who are working in their yards or hanging out on the streets.

These conversations become more open over time, and the prayer walker is enabled to discover more about the neighborhood as well as practice friendship evangelism as the relationship grows.

Get to Know Your Niche

Once you've perused your neighborhood and have gotten to know your neighbors, authentic contextualization requires that you determine which niche you fit into.

Niche ministry is the place where virtually all under-the-radar emerging churches begin. Every neighborhood has niches, though they are especially noticeable in urban contexts. In the urban setting described earlier, a number of niches were discovered by getting to know the neighbors. There was, of course, the student niche. These were mostly postmodern Generation Xers who were away from home for the first time. Another niche was the working poor who had jobs in the restaurants, thrift stores, and local industries. Another niche was the merchants who didn't actually live in the neighborhood but commuted from nearby. These people were generally more affluent than the neighborhood residents but were also very receptive to ministry in the area. Another niche was the "tribal friends." These folks were young singles and couples who held good jobs outside the neighborhood but chose to live there because they liked the urban context. They sometimes shared homes or apartments with a roommate or two and built their own "tribal" family through their network of friends.

After you discover the various niches in the neighborhood, it is time to decide which one you can most easily relate to. In a perfect world, the niche you choose will be the one you are already a part of. Designing ministries to reach this group, therefore, would be a snap.

Discovering the full context of the ministry area before any model is adopted or adapted is critical to the success of any ministry and especially for an under-the-radar emerging church.

Conclusion

As you finish reading this chapter, you may be ready to conclude that this book is a primer on church planting. However, established churches all over America have been trying to do the Nicodemus thing of rebirthing themselves by reentering the womb and changing their DNA patterns. Well-established, though struggling, churches have been trying to recast themselves as purpose-driven or Willow Creek Association all across America with little thought about what that might look like in their context. We are aware of churches in small rural Midwestern towns who have tried to reach the unchurched in their community by "becoming" Willow Creek Association, seeker-driven churches complete with a band, projection video, and so on only to fall flat on their faces. It's not because the concepts for reaching the unchurched are significantly different in these towns, it's that what works in Chicago Metro doesn't stand a chance in rural Missouri. Small-town dynamics are a lot different than wealthy suburban life where the only neighbors you know are the officers on the homeowners association for your subdivision. Instead of trying to put on a seeker-focused presentation each week, perhaps doing something similar once in a while coupled with making the regular worship services more seeker sensitive might work.

It's really all about context. And that is the other part of the theme for this book. We invite you to take a look at these under-the-radar emerging churches, not to clone them, but to experience something that you probably won't see in your community. And as you look at what is working in Seattle, Long Beach, or Akron, we hope you'll get excited and begin to visualize what might be adaptable in your own community with your own niche.

So, go wild. Get excited. Get inspired. But don't head into the lab to begin your own cloning experiments. Leave that for the scientists. Your job is to see the burgeoning harvest and do something about it.

Take Two

• Have you tried to clone a favorite church? What did you learn?
• If you're not familiar with psychographics or even demographics, go to www.percept1.com/pacific/start.asp.

- How much time do you spend in the community compared to the amount of time you spend in the office or with your parishioners? Try to spend an hour in the community for every hour you spend in the office or with parishioners. Make a journal of how you spend your time the next thirty days to see where you are actually focusing your ministry.

CHAPTER THREE

COMMON GROUND, SEATTLE: FINDING THE SACRED IN THE SECULAR

D riving into Mountlake Terrace is like driving into any one of a hundred suburban neighborhoods in the Seattle Metro region. Older homes, by Pacific Northwest standards, built in the 1950s and '60s flank the streets with second and third cars parked out front next to the curbs. While there isn't a Volvo in sight, swing sets, bicycles, and basketball hoops landscape most of the yards. These are the "starter homes" of yesteryear that have become the rental properties of today.

It is in this transitional neighborhood that Common Ground is housed in a converted elementary school building The windows to the main auditorium have been covered and the hanging ceiling tiles removed to reveal pipes, ducts, and electrical conduits creating an industrial atmosphere. Inside the auditorium, several couches and easy chairs are tastefully arranged and rows of stacking chairs are set up and ready to receive the expected crowd of seventy-five to a hundred people.

The lighting is subdued in the room, and the band is warming up on stage. Several small pockets of people are sitting and chatting here and there until Greg Gorsuch, the pastor, steps up to the microphone and welcomes the crowd. The lights dim slightly, and the evening's presentation begins.

Trying to decide what emerging church model to label Common Ground could be an exercise in futility. The church runs a bit like a cell church—small groups are like spokes intentionally connected to the bimonthly presentations that serve as the hub of the church's activities.

On the other hand, Common Ground feels a lot like a minia-ture Willow Creek weekend. The presentations are thoroughly seeker focused. The music tends to be secular tunes done very well, and the themes are of specific interest to an unchurched audience.

Finally, the church feels like a postmodern expression of wor-ship. The video collages they produce, marrying music and film shorts, create an atmosphere of artistic wonder. The setting is subdued and comfortable with living room seating and candles. And the younger crowd espouse an edgy worldview.

We asked Gorsuch what to call the model. He seemed puzzled by the question, but, after some thought, he said the model fit their theology. "You might call it something like an integrative transcendent-immanent model. We're trying to do what Bonhoeffer was suggesting as a secular theology. We concentrate on the intersection between the church and culture. I guess we might call Common Ground a Secular Church model."

Let There Be "Indigenousity"

Indigenous: Originating and living or occurring naturally in an area or environment.
—dictionary.com[1]

The story goes that when missionaries landed in Papua New Guinea, they discovered that making Christianity relevant to the population was going to be challenging. For one, the predomi-nant agricultural pursuit found in the Bible simply made no sense to the residents there. The tale of brave little David, the shepherd who became a mighty warrior, wasn't going to work because the residents there had never seen or heard of an animal called a sheep. Undaunted, the missionaries set out to communicate the gospel in the best way they knew how: by adopting and adapting the metaphors of the people. And in John 1:29 the rough English translation became: "Behold, the pig of God who takes away the sin of the world."[2]

For years the American church has been diligent in preparing missionaries like those in Papua New Guinea for deployment. Before a missionary gets their plane ticket they have studied the language, researched the culture, and considered how to present the gospel in a new land. If they succeed, the missionaries are able to start indigenous churches, churches that are in tune with those around them.

Today one of the biggest mission fields in the world is our own backyard. But the church has often been ineffective in reaching its neighbors because it hasn't done the work of figuring out how to become indigenous to its own culture.

That's exactly where Common Ground has excelled. The leadership team at Common Ground is adept at looking for metaphors in our own culture and finding the reflection of Jesus. Every couple of weeks, the team puts together a multimedia presentation of the gospel that uses images and music few would consider sacred. Clips from movies like *Empire in the Sun* combined with Eric Clapton's "Lonely Stranger" in a multilayered collage stimulate both the senses and the emotions. It's more than "PowerPoint meets slick graphics," and it's more than "*Final Cut Pro* meets mp3s." Instead, the leadership team is committed to searching out where the gospel is already fermenting in the culture's metaphors and icons and then making the effort to clarify the imbedded gospel for their audience.

Paul wrote to the Romans that God was clearly evident in creation.[3] The same can be said of culture. The music we listen to, the movies we watch, the books we read, and the art we appreciate often have God's fingerprints all over them. Like Saint Innocent of Irkutsk, the Common Ground leadership team has studied the culture and borrowed its images to illuminate the message of Jesus Christ.

Finding Jesus in Culture

Each week the Common Ground leadership team meets to look beyond tradition and into the culture itself for a means to the end. Poring over song lyrics, paintings, and a nearly endless supply of movie clips, the team mines the materials in hopes of discovering a few nuggets of the gospel imbedded in culture. The meeting itself is often a tense sparring ground as ideas fly across the room, but, in the end, a theme and message are fashioned. For instance, one week the theme was "the heart of the father." To illuminate the point, the team married the 1998 film version of *Les Miserable* with Clannad's "I Will Find You" and then super-imposed it over Rembrandt's *Prodigal Son* for a collage that left a hush over the audience.

Gorsuch himself is unafraid to look for useful metaphors, images, and the fingerprints of God almost anywhere. He tells the story of watching the Stanley Kubrick movie *Eyes Wide Shut*. "Most married couples would benefit from this movie. It does a better job of exposing the way husbands objectify their wives than any sermon I've ever heard. When I saw the movie I realized that on at least some level I as well as all men sexually objectify their wives." He went on to say that the church has to get honest with culture: "If you hide from it, it is unlikely you can be used to help redeem it."

Presenting Jesus to Culture

The bimonthly presentation at Common Ground is just that, a presentation. They do not consider the events to be worship services in the traditional sense. The presentations are meant to be the fuel for reflective thought. Common Ground tries to create a gestalt moment with each presentation, an "aha!" that illuminates a single facet of God. "We're trying to add one part to the whole rather than trying to explain the whole." Transformed lives don't tend to occur with a single conversion moment but take place by degrees (2 Corinthians 3:18). The Common Ground presentations take advantage of this axiom by what might be considered hyperfocusing on a single theme.

Most of their two-hour presentations include several well-performed songs with stylized multimedia presentations that include the lyrics for those who'd like to sing along; a video segment, typically matched with music; and two or three speakers who address the theme in some tangential manner. The leadership team is committed to illuminating the theme indirectly, taking seriously Fred Craddock's principle of "overhearing the

24

gospel."[4] The effect on the participants is similar to being basted gently in an oven until you're medium-well. The presentation is meant to overwhelm you with imagery but subtly reveal the theme on a subconscious level. It takes some mental dexterity and reflection to connect the dots between the individual parts of the presentation, but that's exactly the point. Gorsuch intends for the participants to leave with more questions than answers. Worship and the reflection on questions are meant to happen in the numerous small groups Common Ground sponsors.

"Much of the spiritual encounter happens a day or two after the presentation—it only begins here." —Greg Gorsuch

This immersion factor, which can seem overwhelming, is the key to the Common Ground model. The bimonthly event is designed to be a catalyst for conversations, which is what separates Common Ground from the typical cell church. In the cell-church model, a cell group's agenda generally include Bible studies, prayer, or some other small group activity. Typically all the cells are brought together weekly for an exciting joint worship service that is meant to unite and galvanize the church.

At Common Ground, however, the central event is designed as a thematic presentation of some aspect of the gospel. It is not worship, and it isn't designed to motivate the church to "get out there and win one for the Lord." Common Ground presents the gospel themes in such a way as to evoke a spiritual unrest, an uneasiness that demands reflection. One of the unwritten goals of the church is that this inner reflection will lead the seeker to participate in one of the small groups where they can wrestle with their questions in a safe environment.

One of the small groups meets immediately following the presentation so that those who have burning questions and issues can find a ready place to express their emotions and wrestle with their questions. However, Gorsuch says that the after-session small group doesn't tend to have the depth of discussion as the ones that meet later in the week since they haven't taken the time to assimilate and reflect on the presentation. The rest of the groups meet later during the week, and not always to discuss the program; indeed, these groups may not broach the topic at all. According to Gorsuch, "When the subject comes up, it bubbles up naturally in the conversations." None of the small groups have a church-imposed agenda. Rather, each chooses the format and purpose of its gathering.

The lack of a church-imposed agenda creates a climate of safety for reflection, for asking questions, and for expressing concerns. No one in the small group is expected to have the answers to whatever issue may arise.

These "safe" environments are critical in Common Ground's Seattle context. In a newspaper ad, the slogan "Churches that have all the answers don't allow questions" reflects the cynicism of the community at large. For too long, traditional churches have supplied simplistic answers to complex questions and have shut down dialogue that calls into question Western values that can be confused with authentic Christianity. Common Ground small groups are meant to be safe environments that offer an opportunity to authentically wrestle with the issues without judgment and often without comment. Rather than answers, leaders and participants offer perspectives, anecdotes, and even ask more questions. The goal isn't to go away with the orthodox correct answer but to leave with a sense of God's grace and a chance to try out answers in real time.

Critique

Every model of church has its strengths and flaws. As church planters, we sometimes find ourselves wed to the model or the style of church we've started and can become blind, or at least myopic, to the shortcomings of what we're doing. There are no perfect churches, and there are no perfect models. Instead we have the opportunity to look, discern, and learn from each.

Strengths

In today's emerging churches there is a propensity of embracing either a low-tech worship style that includes acoustic, chant, and other nonelectronic forms of worship or a high-tech style that uses whatever latest technology is available. Common Ground, however, has found a marriage of both. The setting is absolutely low-tech and has a sacred feel to it on the inside. The warehouse look, married to subdued lighting and comfortable furnishings, creates a hushed atmosphere that evokes a feeling of reverence. On the other hand, when the worship begins, Gorsuch and the leadership team put together high-tech presentations that are professional quality. This combination is nearly perfect for the community context they are trying to reach: a laid-back crowd of people who live, breathe, and work in "computer land."

Gorsuch has done more than serve lattes in the foyer and run a PowerPoint presentation during worship in an attempt to be "authentic" to the context. He has taken the pulse of his community by spending an inordinate amount of time studying and getting to know his neighbors until he knows intuitively what will work and what won't. This kind of intuition is born of hard work and significant time spent with the unchurched and the irreligious. There are no shortcuts to being authentically indigenous, and Common Ground has done their work well.

Weaknesses

An inherent danger lies just under the surface when one goes about mining culture for God. Just as pentecostal churches have been accused of finding a demon underneath every rock, a similar accusation could be made of churches who try to find Jesus beneath every cultural image. If the attempt to find Jesus in culture is pushed to the extreme, there is a danger that the gospel can become so watered down that it is rendered essentially meaningless. Further, if God is "discovered" and pointed out in too many unfortunate contexts, those who are outside the church may start to accuse us of seeing God not beneath but *in* every rock. Effectively presenting the sacred to culture through cultural metaphor and image must be handled carefully. Common Ground will have to watch closely to ensure that they do not make this mistake.

Although the word *community* is overused almost to the point of losing its significance, without it there may be a worship service but no authentic church. Common Ground has several opportunities for people to "plug in" and become a part of the church community, but these opportunities seem to take a backseat to the bimonthly presentation. When I (BTB) was there, it was apparent that there were three small groups that were active in the congregation. Only one of those groups intentionally focused on the theme of the presentation; the other two relied on it "bubbling up" from the collective subconscious.

Following a presentation service there is a need for intentional reflection, discipling, and worship opportunities. Although Gorsuch and the leadership team produce a high-tech Eucharist service several times each year, this would be more effective if at least part of the worship component were shifted into a small group setting that married the bimonthly theme to a high touch community home worship.

Another potential weakness in the Common Ground model is in their small group model. Common Ground has two opportunities for implanting the DNA into the congregation at large: during the presentations and during the small-group time. Although it is clear that the behavior of the leadership reflects the core values, there seems to be little emphasis on imparting that DNA to the congregation at large. Because small groups are intimate and provide an opportunity for teaching and discussion, this would seem to be the most likely venue for infusing the DNA. However, because the small groups are apparently autonomous, at least when it comes to their programming, the opportunity to instill the mission, vision, and values of the larger community is lost. In our experience, without implanting the DNA firmly in the minds, hearts, and behaviors of the participants, the congregation could be in danger of schism, factioning, and strife.

What We Learned

- Whether art imitates life or the other way around, it's important to take seriously the themes of popular culture. If it has found its way into popular culture, it is important that Christians take off their blinders and explore the issues behind it. Remember what Gorsuch said: "If you hide from it, it is unlikely you can be used to help redeem it."

- Don't be afraid to poke and prod beneath the surface of cultural icons, metaphors, and arts to find the fingerprint of God. You never know what you'll find that you can adapt, adopt, and present. How the Apostle Paul handled his opportunity to share the gospel at Mars Hill is still a valid example for us today. Paul first spent some time studying the city's culture. He discovered not only that the city was full of idols but also that there was a predominate atmosphere of curiosity that fueled discussion and debate. So, from reading the culture, he used their "unknown God" as the point of departure for his presentation of the gospel. Paul was in a totally different culture when he arrived in Athens, and he knew that the best way to be heard was to address his audience through some facet of their culture (Acts 17). Since we are entering a very different culture from the past five hundred years of Protestant history, we should do the same.[5]

- Being indigenous to the culture in which a church finds itself takes large amounts of time (by *indigenous* we mean in the language, techology, and culture of the people you are trying to reach). Given the vast changes over the past few decades, Christians can no longer assume they understand the culture around them, especially if they have been a Christian for some time. In addition, our culture is changing so fast that trying to be indigenous is a full-time task. There are no shortcuts in getting to know the hearts and souls of your neighbors.

- Churches of all sizes can produce high-tech art that rivals what they produce in Hollywood. Don't settle for mediocre. Your audience won't.

- Of course the question emerges, *after the previous point of not settling for mediocrity has been made, how do you get all these artists and technicians to "join up"?* The answer isn't found in a church office or a committee meeting. Discovering local talent is generally found in relationships built outside the church. Gorsuch has put together an incredible worship and arts team from those folks he has rubbed shoulders with in the local culture. From night clubs to art shows, he has built relationships with artists of virtually all stripes and has invited them to work on projects that can make a difference in people's lives at Common Ground. Sure, there's lots of skepticism at first when he starts talking about church and Common Ground, but because he offers them a venue in which they can shine and because they have come to trust him, they often throw their lot in with him and their contributions are what make the difference.

- Emerging churches are aware that transformation is often more of a process than a decision. This is especially true in the Northwest due to the prevailing cynicism toward organized religion. However, emerging churches place far more emphasis on relationships that have to be built and nurtured before people are willing to hear one's personal faith story, much less the biblical story. The shift from people coming to worship to find God to people finding God and then coming to worship is one of the most profound shifts of our lifetime.
- The Secular Church model could become a highly effective model for reaching the unchurched as long as more emphasis is placed on the cell groups where community could be built, worship would be central, and the presentation's theme would be woven into the fabric of the small group.
- We should also note that studies show that a growing number of younger people prefer smaller churches rather than the large megachurch crowd. So, one of the ways churches reach more people and remain intimate is through small groups.[6]

What's Different about Common Ground?

(Response from Greg Gorsuch, Pastor of Common Ground)

"I will put my law within them, and I will write it on their hearts; ... and they shall be my people"—many "people," each individual unique, not a homogenized collective, but a celebration of difference under the unity of Christ. "No longer shall they teach one another, or say to each other, 'Know the LORD,' for they shall all know me, from the least of them to the greatest, says the LORD; for I will forgive their iniquity, and remember their sin no more."[7] For the writer of Hebrews, this is the nature of the "new covenant." The old covenant "is obsolete and growing old will soon disappear."[8]

What does the writer mean, that each will know God from within his or her own heart? Furthermore, why is the new covenant still "becoming," given that the resurrection and Pentecost have already happened? Possibly, the entire history of the church represents the steady movement from king-teacher-law authority toward that of individuals under the authority of one Spirit, each knowing Christ more personally and each within their own story. The history of the church, in fact, does reveal ongoing stages of reformation and expansion in the way we know God.

At Common Ground, we aspire to what I would call genuine postmodern communications, which is ultimately still impossible. Most emerging church models represent smaller tribes in which worship and the gospel are experienced similarly within the group as a whole, which may be real and good, but which is not what I would consider postmodern. The goal of Common Ground is to speak through a confluence of cultural and sacred art in such a way that the word and sacrament of Christ are *multitribal*—each individual, sex, age, or group connecting to the experience in ways that are most meaningful to them. This is done by painting in broad impressionistic strokes of art and story, sacred and secular, in ways that draw individuals more deeply into an experience that is personally meaningful for each. It is felt more deeply than when the collective is forced to experience the same thing. Hollywood knows how to do this; the church is failing (moviegoing versus church attendance).

Common Ground also attempts to enter the heart as deeply as possible before encountering the truth and grace of Christ. By employing the art of our culture we are able to crack open areas in our lives that have long since been closed for "safety's" sake. Appropriate use of film, drama, and story/lyrics allows the gospel to penetrate into areas not otherwise allowed.

Fred Craddock tells us, "The parable is the example par excellence of a piece of literature that is not designed to convey information but by its very form arrests the attention, draws the listener into personal involvement, and leaves the final resolution of the issue to the hearer's own judgment."[9] This is the goal of Common Ground. Each service, presentation, and small-group discussion, as well as our ongoing interaction with the

31

world, is done in such a way as to live and communicate with enough room for Christ to speak personally and meaningfully to each.

Take Two

- What opportunities can you think of to immerse yourself in the culture around you?
- How much time do you spend in these opportunities for the purpose of interpreting the culture to yourself and those around you so that it can find its way into your worship?
- What parts of culture do you think would be either off-limits or too radical for your congregation?
- What parts of culture did Jesus embrace that might have been considered off-limits or too radical by the Pharisees and Sadducees?
- To learn more about Common Ground go to www.common-groundseattle.org where you can find examples of their visual arts as well as a number of reflection papers on what Common Ground presents.

CHAPTER FOUR

ALPHA CHURCH: A COMING OF AGE

B obby" is a full member of Alpha Church. He attends his church every week, sometimes several times during the week. "Bobby" was one of the first to be baptized at Alpha Church. As a young man working in a suburb of Atlanta, he had spoken with the Reverend Patricia E. Walker, the Alpha Church pastor, on many occasions about this day, and he was ready. He had done all she had asked him to do. He had two witnesses by his side. He had invited his family and friends to the big event. He even invited all his coworkers. All the necessary trappings for the event were on his office desk: a Bible, a towel, a basin of water, and the telephone. The big moment came.

On a workday afternoon, during the lunch break, his witnesses and a number of his coworkers crowded into a suburban office as they telephoned Pastor Walker, put her on speakerphone, and proceeded with the ancient rite of baptism. "In the name of the Father, the Son, and the Holy Spirit" came the voice over the phone as the two witnesses poured water over "Bobby's" head. "Bobby's" baptism into the kingdom of God was complete and his membership in Alpha Church, a global cyberchurch, was secure.

There are many church Web sites on the Internet. A recent Google search for "church Web sites" returned more than 3.8 million sites; however, most church Web sites hardly qualify as a cyberchurch. In our definition, a full-service cyberchurch is a church without walls that "meets" electronically for worship, evangelism, relationship building, discipleship, and empowerment to do good

---

works of service. A full-service cyberchurch accomplishes everything that the typical church can accomplish including communion, baptisms, offerings, sermons, singing, and so on. To date, we've only discovered one full-service cyberchurch online—Alpha Church at www.alphachurch.org.

The Inevitable

It was only a matter of time before someone figured out how to go to the next level of Internet connectivity for the church. Alpha Church was the brainchild of Patricia Walker and her brother Rob, both of whom were United Methodist pastors. They were attending a conference where Leonard Sweet was keynoting. In his presentation he spoke of the power and the future of the Internet, and his words stuck in Patricia's mind. Later that day, she attended a Web site training workshop and realized she was a natural at using and producing Web site content. A conversation with her brother settled the issue: she would launch a cyberchurch.

Patricia Walker left the United Methodist Church in order to launch the church, but she was committed to remaining an accountable leader. So she put together a board to ensure adequate oversight, filed the required 501(c)(3) paperwork in order to be a "real" church in the eyes of the IRS, and started taking classes in Web site development.

At first, she did most of the design work on her own, but as she began to develop the site, she also developed a network of supporters. "I met a couple of paraplegics online who gave me lots of advice on what was needed for an Internet church," she said. Walker solicited and incorporated advice from a wide audience. Her mother suggested cyber baptism while pondering a thought she had about people in China who couldn't otherwise get baptized. She's heard from a number of folks who deal with various levels of autism about the need for visuals on the site.

Equipped with her own ideas, suggestions from a wider audience, and guidance from her board, Walker designed and developed the Web site format and uploaded it in 1999. In just a couple of years, the site went from conception to more than one-and-a-half million

Internet hits. Alpha Church, at the time of this publication, has about six-thousand participants and more than one hundred members from all over the world. "People join the church in waves. Lately people have been joining the church from Canada."[1]

The Online Community

There have been some concerns about the online community. Is there really such a thing as a community if the people never see each other, let alone share space together? Can a community exist that consists only of patterned ones and zeros traveling thousands of miles through copper and fiber optics?

Apparently, the answer is a qualified yes. The sheer rise of cyber communities on the Internet suggests the need exists. Alpha Church is certainly not the first cyber community on the Web. The first cyberchurch that got national press was zchurch.com. The church sported a cartoonlike quality until recently—a highly technical cartoonlike quality, but cartoonlike nonetheless. Later, www.theooze.com, www.wuzupgod.com, and www.easumbandy.com gained popularity as online communities as well.

These cyberchurches were as near to full-service community churches as one could imagine at the time, though none offered the sacraments electronically. However, what they did offer filled a need that the church down the street didn't.

The Cyberchurch Tour

Before we begin our tour of Alpha Church, it's important to point out the difference between a cyberchurch and a church Web site. Most churches of any size today have a Web site. These Web sites tend to exist for two or three purposes: (1) to market the church; (2) to keep its members informed of upcoming events; and (3) to share the good news with those who have not heard. A cyberchurch site, on the other hand, exists in order to gather, facilitate, and support an online community of Christian disciples. To that end, cyberchurch Web sites are highly interactive and tend to have multiple interactive opportunities by community members.

Chat Rooms

Probably the best-known interactive forum on the Internet is the chat room. Introduced in 1988, chat rooms caught on in the late 1990s and today are often coupled with instant messaging (IM). Chat rooms allow multiple online users to "chat" with each other in real time.[2] Most of this chatting is done using the keyboard; however, as broadband technology makes its way into more homes, the use of Web video cameras and audio feeds are becoming more prominent.[3]

Instant messaging is regularly used in the chat rooms to carry on private conversations. IM technology sends a real-time message to a recipient. These messages are not viewable by the general chat room population, thus providing a measure of privacy. It is not uncommon for a participant in a general chat room to be carrying on three or four IM conversations at the same time as they participate in the wider chat room.

The strength of the interactivity of chat rooms is also its chief weakness: it is real-time communication. In a world where those who attend a cyberchurch do so at their own convenience, the need to be online and present in the chat room at an appointed time is a real drawback.

Alpha Church does offer a chat room on their site, although many, if not most, cyberchurches to date have eschewed that particular technology in favor of bulletin boards and blogs.

Bulletin Boards and Blogs

Bulletin board technology has been around for a long time. A bulletin board allows a member of the community to post a message (called a post) onto a Web page that serves as a public proclamation and allows other members of the community to respond to it. An initial posting is often the beginning of a lengthy online conversation, called a thread, that can be responded to by many members of the community. More threads are started whenever a new topic is started by another member of the community.

A blog, on the other hand, is more like an online journal. The word *blog* is a contraction of the words we**b** **log** and has become popular over the past couple of years. Blogs are often open to all the members of the community to post their daily thoughts, whether they be reflections on what God is doing in their lives or their opinions on someone else's thoughts. Blog entries are chronologically rather than topically arranged like the bulletin boards.

In both of these cases, members of the cyberchurch create a community among themselves by participating in the conversations. Often a conversation will begin with a single post that generates interest by a number of folks who post their initial thoughts. As time passes, however, the conversation may continue with only two or three participants who ultimately get to know each other better through the exchanges.

Forums

Online forums are a popular interactive tool for many cyberchurches. Forums work similarly to bulletin boards, except the conversation is carried on by e-mail rather than being posted to a Web page.[4] A member of the forum writes an observation, expresses an opinion, or asks a question and sends it to the forum. All the forum members individually receive the e-mail and can choose whether to respond to the wider forum, where all can join in the conversation, or directly to the writer in a personal e-mail. These forums are popular, in part, because they take advantage of the popularity of e-mail communications.

Polls and Surveys

In recent years, polls and surveys have become quite popular in our nation. Not only have they caught on in the political realm, they're popular interactive devices for reality TV and the Internet. Many cyberchurch Web sites are taking advantage of this tool in order to solicit the opinions of those visiting their sites as well as to entice Web surfers to return to view the results. An online poll or a survey offers the opportunity for a member of the wider online community to be "heard" as well as to provide an occasion for the cyberchurch participant to add his or her input to the mix.

Tip O'Neill, former Speaker of the House, says one of the most important things to remember in politics is that "people like to be asked."[5] Online polls engage those who surf and the Web site, which is why many cyberchurches use the polling software on their site.

The Cyberchurch of the Future

Interactivity is a key to the cyberchurch experience. Today, very few people want to sit and be preached at; they want to have input into what's presented. The cyberchurch of the future will take this seriously and adapt developing technology to increase the interconnectivity and interactivity of the online community.

The question is, *what will the future cyberchurch look like?* Walker suggests that the future will include holographic images. "Imagine sitting down with the apostles as they do the teaching in your living room." That may sound far-fetched, but, according to those in the cyberspace realm, it is only a few years away.[6] In *Growing Spiritual Redwoods*, Bill Easum wrote about the Church of the Virtual Resurrection. In that section he imaged what a holographic worship service might look like.[7]

Already, streaming audio and video technology allows face-to-face conversations with little more than a nineteen-dollar webcam and a broadband connection. As the technology improves, multiple webcam video conversations will allow small group worship or other interactions. In the future, streaming conversations from all over the world will be instantly translated aurally for all the participants. And cyberchurch won't be tied to the home computer as PDAs, cell phones, and other mobile devices become more cyber-friendly.[8]

Just as Martin Luther and John Wesley would hardly recognize the church of today, it's difficult to imagine what our churches will look like tomorrow. But whatever may happen, technology and the cyberchurch will be a part of the key.

Creating Cyberchurch

Creating a cyberchurch is a time-intensive task. Although keeping a local church's Web site updated may only take an hour or so each week, becoming the pastor of a cyberchurch is not unlike being the pastor of a more traditional church—there are always more things to do than there are hours in the day. Our first recommendation is, if you're thinking about launching a cyberchurch, consider how to raise support for a full-time cyberpastor. This isn't a part-time job.

Before you begin, you'll want to have an idea of what services you'll want on your Web site. If you will be providing a weekly online worship service, what will that look like? Will it be a "live" service using a video camera, or will it be a Macromedia Flash sermon like the ones Walker provides at Alpha Church? Will your site be highly interactive with chat rooms, bulletin boards, blogs, surveys, and so on? If so, make a note that you will need CGI script access. Will your site offer streaming video? If so, note that you will need an internet host with 7,200 rpm or faster hard drives, and you will also need large capacity for your files, probably 100 megabytes or more. Knowing in advance what you hope to offer on your Web site will ensure you sign up for the right Internet services the first time. Finally, how are you going to solicit funding?[9] If the Web site will collect tithes and offerings, how will you do that? You'll also need to decide how the money will be handled.

To create a cyberchurch, there is quite of list of to-dos besides designing and running the Web site. The list below will get you started.

1. Choose a unique domain name for your Web site.

A domain name is the main part of a Web site's URL (Uniform Resource Locator) and is essentially a leased address, that is, you "own" it so long as you pay an annual fee for it. You can find out if your name is available at most Web site registration sites. Don't forget there are new Web site extensions being released such as .info and .tv, and more are being added to keep up with the demand for unique domain names.

2. Choose an affordable host who will provide adequate service for your Web site.

A host is a Web server who will store your Web pages on their computers and make them available so anyone online can find them. There are plenty of hosts out there, but prices can range from more than $100 per month to less than $10 per month, so shop around. If you're a novice, it will pay to make sure the host has good tech support—you'll probably need it.

3. Purchase the domain name and get the site set up on your host's server.

When you've chosen your host, it's time to purchase your domain name. Contact your host, and with credit card in hand, place your order and have them set your site up on their server. This typically takes about twenty-four hours, but don't worry: it will be days before you're ready to launch your site anyway.

4. Design your site.

Design your Web site with your intended visitor in mind. Most folks using the Internet are looking for information, and if they don't see what they're looking for on the front page, or else through an easy link, they often surf away to the next site. Your home page has to catch their attention long enough to draw them in. Also, don't forget: interactive, interactive, interactive. That's the only way an online church member can gain a sense of community.

5. Build your site using an HTML editor.

You will probably need to be familiar with CGI scripts, JavaScript, and Flash in order to build an interactive site. Build your site using an HTML editor. If you're an expert in HTML (Hyper Text Markup Language, the language of the Internet), then the only software you'll need is a basic text editor like Microsoft Notepad. Most, however, use software that automatically does most of the coding. There are a number of great software programs to assist in your Web page development. You will also probably need to do some Flash programming for animated webshots, install CGI scripts for bulletin boards, hit counters, and surveys, and be familiar with using JavaScript for dynamic data and graphics displays. Building a Web site is not for the technologically ignorant.

6. Upload your site onto your host's server.

Upload your site using your HTML editor (most have upload as one of the features), or else use an FTP manager.

7. Test the site.

There is nothing more infuriating to a Web surfer than "Error 404: Page Cannot Be Found" errors. Make sure all your scripts run, all your graphics load, and all your pages can be found.

8. Advertise the Web site through search engines, e-mails to friends and family, and other marketing ideas you may choose to employ.

Getting a site advertised online used to be a rather simple task. Simply let Yahoo, AltaVista, and Lycos know that you exist, and they would link your site to their search engine. Times have changed and with literally billions of Web pages out there, getting listed on a search engine can be a bit more difficult. The easiest way is to simply pay your way onto the main search engines or to hire someone to provide you with Web page optimization services. Yahoo, Google, and others all provide listing services for a fee, and it's the only way to guarantee you'll get your site listed. Other ways to market your site is to let people know by e-mail, but don't spam anyone; just let your friends know. Don't forget the news groups. There are many groups out there, and a quickly posted note can generate a number of hits on your Web site. And finally, don't forget more traditional marketing opportunities such as advertising in local newspapers, and so on.

9. Keep up with site maintenance.

Maintaining a Web site is like raising a child: the task is ongoing and never really done. As people get involved they will need new opportunities for interaction and to build their online community. A site that doesn't get a face-lift fairly often is destined for obscurity, so plan on upgrading your site's general design at least annually.

Critique

Like anything new, the cyberchurch has its advocates and its opponents. There are many questions that only time and observation will answer. Does the cyberchurch foster or fetter relationships? Is cyber worship a lone act or a community exercise? Is cybermentoring effective in making committed disciples of Jesus? How much of a challenge does the cyberchurch offer to the located church? Is a cyberchurch a stand-alone congregation, or is it better suited as a ministry of a local church? Can cyberchurch become truly evangelistic? We won't know the answers to these questions for some time. But one thing is certain: whatever answers we find in the future, the cyberchurch will be part of that future.

Strengths

At this moment, the cyberchurch offers the only opportunity for an inclusive international church. Alpha Church has participants from nearly every continent. Some members of the international community participate from behind closed doors because the practice of Christianity in their nation is an unsafe option. Others join the cyberchurch because it offers the best option for active participation in their community. One member of the Alpha Church community logs on from a cyber café every week in order to be active in a church.

A second strength of the cyberchurch is that it speaks the language of an image-driven culture. Walker creates a Flash production every week for Alpha Church. This production is image driven and never relies on a talking head. Most cyberchurches rely on Flash, streaming video, streaming audio, as well as any number of interactive opportunities in order to reach and hold the attention of their Web surfing congregation. Computerese is more than just the language of so called computer geeks, it's now the language of much of the world, and cyberchurch speaks the language better than any other organized religion to date.

One possible strength of the cyberchurch is its potential to share the good news inexpensively and in hard to reach places. On a plane ride a few years ago, Bill E. was talking to one of his young pastor friends who is known for being slightly off-the-wall. Bill asked him what he was doing new. He replied, "We're training our cyber monkeys to be undercover spiritual avatars who invade popular chat rooms for the purpose of sharing the gospel. It's amazing how open the conversations are about spiritual issues that often lead to the Christ question." However, as we will see in the next section, what could be a strength usually turns out to be a weakness.

Weaknesses

Probably the most serious weakness of the cyberchurch has been its ineffectiveness in reaching non-Christians. Walker admits that most of those who visit the Alpha Church Web site are already Christians who are looking to find something more than what they are currently experiencing in their spiritual lives. It is unlikely that many non-Christians are dropping into cyber-churches for a quick spirituality fix. So far, those who *do* drop in, regularly do so to deride organized religion. Their handiwork can be seen occasionally on the cyberchurch's public bulletin boards. Seldom do we read of people coming to Christianity as a result of a Christian Web site.

However, the potential for evangelism is still present in the cyberchurch. A close look at Alpha Church reveals that there isn't much there to attract the non-Christian or to bring them into their church when doing a search of the Web. We still feel that if more attention were given to reaching the non-Christian, the cyberchurch could offer a fertile field for evangelism.

A second weakness is the charge that cyberchurches undermine real relationships. Cocooning is a serious issue in our culture. Many folks can go all day without physically interacting with a single human being. In most places, we can pump our gas and pay for it without talking to anyone, buy our groceries and use the self-checkout lanes, and so on. Cyberchurch provides yet another opportunity to avoid human contact altogether. This also provides an excuse for not getting personally involved in evangelism, doing works of service for others, or being personally called into accountability. What isn't clear at the moment is the effect of virtual reality and holographic imaging on the future of cyber worship and small groups. We are not yet ready to pass judgment either way but feel the church must be open to the possibility that even the nature and essences of reality itself may be undergoing a remarkable conversion.

Besides the potential of undermining real relationships, another question for the cyberchurch begs the issue of virtual reality. The trilogy *The Matrix* illuminates this point as it creates a computer programmed reality for all humanity. Some would suggest that this is already a present phenomenon for those who have become addicted to both video games and/or computer chat rooms.

Finally, with the exception of those providing the code for the cyberchurch, there is little commitment required by members of the cyber community. Perhaps there are those who do tithe or give significant offerings to support the cyberchurch; however, these would be the exception, not the rule. Besides financial support of the church, there is little else required of the cyberchurch member; indeed, there is little else a cyberchurch member can actually do to get involved unless they happen to have HTML, Flash, or some other cyber language skill.

We suggest that cyberchurches of the future provide and promote local gatherings of their members and participants. Such gatherings would be a simple step to accomplish. First, all of the participants within a hundred miles could be invited to attend the monthly worship or fellowship or mission project. Once gathered, one of the participants being mentored by the cyberchurch fills the role of pastor and facilitates the event. By hosting events like these, the cyberchurch would be providing ongoing mentorship of future leaders, creating more intimate relationships, and achieving a visible mission presence that would become an inspiration for other groups to attempt.[10]

What We Learned

- Cyberchurch is more than just another church Web site. Most churches use their Web sites for self-promotion in order to gather visitors from local Web surfers. A full-service cyberchurch offers virtually every service that a local church offers. Some would say that the cyberchurch cannot offer authentic relationships and community. We disagree. Communities are being formed online almost daily. Just look at sites like eBay, and take into consideration how many people are finding a spouse through online dating and matching services. In a digital world, even the concepts of community and relationships are being stretched.

- One of the reasons for the popularity of the cyberchurch is its interactivity. In our society, people want to have some sort of input into what's transpiring in front of them. Whether it's a simple poll, a bulletin board, or an opportunity to chat, interactivity is a requirement for today's online community. We think this is a lesson the typical local church needs to learn, not just for its own Web sites but in its worship and its programming. Today's generation is less willing to sit and be lectured to. They want to interact, to connect, to hear, and to be heard. Whether the church decides to invest in wireless Internet or Intranet connectivity so guests and members alike can interact using their laptops or PDAs during the weekly sermon or other programming, or simply to open up the "sermon time" and other programs to input, questions, and comments from the congregation doesn't seem to matter as much as providing the opportunity.

• The cyberchurch is probably the only truly inclusive church on the planet, offering a level playing field for anyone with access to a computer. In cyberspace everyone who gets connected is close to equal. Some may have the latest equipment or a faster broadband connection, but in Paul's words, "There is no longer Jew or Greek, there is no longer slave or free, there is no longer male and female" (Galatians 3:28). Unless you turn on your webcam, when you're online no one knows whether you are wealthy or poor; American or Asian; black, white, red, yellow, or a rich mocha brown; young or old; sick or well; and no one knows if you're in a wheelchair or if you're a marathon runner. Participants of the cyberchurch come to their church in the same way they come to the throne of grace: unencumbered by anything except what they carry in their heart. On the other hand anonymity can also be a negative, and people in cyber relationships have to exercise extreme caution.

• Planting a full-service cyberchurch demands at least the same amount of time as a church planter doing an urban, suburban, or rural plant. When Alphachurch was in its infancy, Walker would spend as much as four long days developing each of her weekly Flash sermons to publish online. Today it only takes one very long day to produce it, but as technology changes, she has to continually upgrade her education and her equipment. Further, being pastor of a full-service cyberchurch is a full-time job once the congregation is established. And although no one was willing to share whether or not their cyberchurch was providing full-time financial funding, it is unlikely that cyberchurch members are more financially committed to their church than their more traditional church counterparts.

Conclusion

One word best describes the cyberchurch: *potential*. The world of cyberspace has only just been discovered and a vast untouched and unimagined wilderness is awaiting exploration. The cyber-church is not just doing the reconnaissance work, it's blazing the trail for those who will follow. Whether the cyberchurch will become an extension of the local church or a mission of the international church is yet to be seen, but the potential for reaching the world through the Internet is very real indeed.

Take Two

- The cyberchurch offers its members inclusive connectivity. What opportunities can you think of that would allow you to connect with those who might otherwise feel excluded by the church?
- What could be done in your worship experience to provide more interactivity?
- What would happen if you set up an Alpha Church–style Web site for your congregations rather than the typical Web site you may have now? How would that affect your ministries?
- What ways can you think of to capitalize on the strengths of the Internet without the medium becoming the message?
- How did Jesus connect with the disconnected and excluded people of his day?
- How could your church increase its interconnectivity with you and with those who are not well connected?

CHAPTER FIVE

IMAGO DEI: RENAISSANCE, ART, AND MONASTICISM

If you're looking for glitz, glimmer, and all new, then the Imago Dei Community in Portland, Oregon, is not where you want to begin. Stepping into the Old Laurelhurst Church building where they meet for worship is like stepping into another century. There is clearly a narthex and a nave; the ceiling architectural beams look like you've walked into an upside-down sailing ship with all the futtocks and ribs exposed. There are neither stacking nor theater chairs, but old polished pews to sit on during worship. All in all, it doesn't look like the kind of place you'd expect to see 500 twenty- and thirty-somethings coming for church. But each week, divided among three Sunday services, that's exactly what happens.

On the other hand, ancient-future doesn't quite describe Imago Dei either. When the worship starts, the band cranks out urban grunge tunes indigenous to the Pacific Northwest. It's loud, rock-and-roll, and heartfelt. The words to the tunes are projected on the wall—poorly, because the walls weren't designed for PowerPoint presentations. There are a few candles, but, with the exception of the building's architecture, there's nothing gothic about what's going on here—not so much as a chant in the house.

What's remarkable enough about Imago Dei that it warrants our attention? It's their seamless wedding of arts in culture and monasticism, a marriage we call Renaissance, Art, and Monasticism.

In the fourteenth century, the Renaissance began as a rebirth of the culture. A renewal of interest in the arts and sciences caused medieval thinkers to rethink their worldview. And though it took a couple of centuries before the church experienced its own

47

rebirth, it was arguably the Renaissance artists and their art that began to subtly change the heartscapes within the church.

Today, many emerging churches have learned to incorporate artists and their art into the worship. It is not uncommon to hear original music, to view original video clips, or even to watch artists at work during the worship service. What makes Imago Dei unique is the way they have woven the arts and artists into the DNA of their community.

Imago Dei is a daughter church of Acts 29 Network, a ministry partnership between David Nicholas at Spanish River Presbyterian in Boca Raton, Florida, and Mark Driscoll at Mars Hill, Seattle, Washington. Pastor Rick McKinley applied to the Acts 29 Network as a church planter, and, in January 2000, he arrived in Portland to begin his work. Imago Dei launched in October of 2000 with fifty in attendance, and though they have avoided commercial marketing, they continually attract a growing congregation.

Art in the Church

For many congregations, art is little more than an additional program appended to the church's *real* business. Historically, however, the arts have been much more important to the church's purpose. Early in the church's history, icons were used as "windows to the divine." These little "pictures" invited the worshiper to contemplate the mysteries of the faith by gazing upon the heroes and saints of the church. Similarly, frescoes and mosaics of saints and religious scenes adorned the walls of the early church buildings. And later, cathedrals were built with commissioned stained glass windows that became literal portals to the divine. These windows told the stories of scripture both to those who could not read and to those who simply appreciated their beauty. At the same time handwritten copies of scriptures became ornate *objets d'art* as scribes became calligraphers who became graphic artists with pen and ink. During this period, the church grew tremendously across Asia, Europe, and Northern Africa.

Arts continued to be an important aspect of the church through the Middle Ages and even into the Enlightenment. However, as the Modern period emerged, asthetics were eclipsed by intellectualism and rational thought became the church's credo. Arts in the church were disdained and became one of the Reformation's casualties. The empty cross became the sole icon of Protestantism; all other icons of the saints, and even the saints themselves, were banished from the church. Unadorned communion tables replaced ornate altars. Religious paintings found themselves hanging in galleries and estates rather than gracing sanctuaries. Appreciation of art was vanquished to avoid emotionalism creeping into the faith.

Today, however, the emerging church is experiencing the birth pangs of a renaissance in the arts. With the crumbling of the Modern period and with the glorification of the intellect waning, the arts have begun to find their way back into the church. Whereas, during much of the Modern era, new hymns were introduced into the churches infrequently, today whole new genres of music have taken many, if not most, of our churches by storm. Technology has added the possibility of arts on the big screen, and many emerging churches have excelled in this new art. And even murals, paintings, and sculptures have been reintroduced in some church buildings—arts that would have been banned from the house of God only a few years ago.

Art as Lifestyle

From the beginning, the arts have been an important part of Imago Dei, being woven seamlessly throughout the whole church, whereas, in most churches, the addition of the arts is just that, an addition—something that's tacked on to enhance the program. The intergration of art into the life of the congregation is the key to Imago Dei and its ministry. Art isn't an add-on, it's who they are. Worship and beauty is one of their core values, and they manifest this value in every aspect of the church.

> *"For us, art is not an expression of a pragmatic task, but an expression of who we are and what God's doing in us."*
> —*Rick McKinley, pastor of Imago Dei*

Because Imago Dei rents the Old Laurelhurst church building for their weekly worship services, setup includes not only hauling in a professional sound system for their worship band but also preparing the artist's corner near the front. During the message, one of their artistic members will attempt to capture on canvas the heart of the gospel presentation. These images aren't simply spontaneous expressions. During the week McKinley and his worship planning team meet and discuss the upcoming service. McKinley attempts to convey what he expects to say during the sermon and tries to inspire the rest of the team to create a wholistic experience through performance and presentation arts. He says, "Art is the subjective that points to the objective. They point to the spiritual reality of what I'm communicating."

Virtually every form of artistic expression is embraced by Imago Dei. On any Sunday you might encounter original music from a variety of genres, dance, drama, computer-generated graphics, video, painting, sculpting, crafts, photography, or oral renderings of the literary arts from poetry to prose.

When asked how they believe their artistic emphasis is reaching the community, they are quick to point out that art is *not* their focus, reaching the community for Christ is. Art subtly accentuates worship, not the other way around. McKinley says incorporating art into the worship helps to reach the lost because it is something they can connect to—the arts are "christocentric windows to the heart."

But art isn't just a value in worship. It's an important part of the very foundation of Imago Dei. For instance, Peter Jenkins, one of the members of Imago Dei, saw the realization of a vision he had for further embracing the arts and artists by the establishment of the Artistery. The Artistery is a monasticlike community for artists who desire to learn the spiritual and artistic disciplines of practicing and refining their art in a Christian environment. The Artistery is a one-year home to five young men who live in a single residence in the Brooklyn arts community in Portland. These artists are required to work at a job outside of the Artistery and to provide a portion of the living expenses. They also share community chores such as cooking, cleaning, and providing simple maintenance. Their monastic-artistic duties include a weekly spiritual group study meeting, attendance at church, and attendance at the monthly Imago Dei potluck fellowship dinner. They must also lead a weekly class in their artistic specialty for the general public, begin and complete a new artistic project each month, and produce a show of their work sometime during their stay. Art from the Artisterians can regularly be viewed on the Imago Dei Community Web site (www.imagodeicommunity.com).

The Artistery began when Peter, the founder, director, and, for all practical purposes, the abbot of the Artistery, experienced Imago Dei's artistic values. He had long entertained a vision of marrying the arts with Christian ministry and believed that artists in the church need to invest their work in the church. He was encouraged by McKinley to pursue his vision, and he set out to find a home for his dream.

Imago Dei supports the Artistery by its values, but the Artistery itself was expected to be fully self-supporting in its ministry. To date, Peter has yet to draw a salary from the Artistery and supports himself as a house painter. The Artistery has been a self-contained and self-sustaining ministry from the beginning and today has a waiting list of artists who want to join the community. Peter hopes to open as many as four other Artisteries over the next few years, including one for women.

Even though McKinley is proud of the Artistery, he is adamant that it is just one of many related to the arts at Imago Dei. And he's careful to say that the artistic ministries are just a part of who Imago Dei is, a community set on reaching the world for Jesus Christ.

Embedding Art in Worship

Unfortunately, many church leaders who visit Imago Dei come away thinking that adding art to worship is the next magic pill that will compel the unchurched to walk through their doors. Invariably, their question is, *how do you get artists to come?*

The answer is less about technique and more about values. Arts can't be just an add-on. It has to well up from the heart and soul of the church itself. One of the chief problems church leaders find themselves in is that the Modern worldview has devalued the experiential and the emotional. At one time beauty and truth were virtually synonymous within the church. However, Modern thinking relegated beauty to the museum and elevated empirical scientific "fact" as ultimate truth. With that kind of attitude, art was generally lost to the church and was replaced with exegetical exposition of the Scriptures. As Neil Cole has said, "We are educated beyond our obedience."[1]

The question we need to be asking is, *how do we revive a value of artistic expression in the church today?* Some church leaders seem to believe that the best way to do this is to go out and attract an artist to start doing "their thing" during the worship service. But convincing a local artist to paint a watercolor during the sermon isn't going to create an embodied value within the congregation. The real issue hinges on the word *revive*. If there hasn't been a shared church value for the arts somewhere in the past, there won't be a revival because there is nothing to revive. Instead, an existing church will have to develop a new value, which is a much more difficult task. Creating a new value means more than just trying to "add" something to what exists. It means that the value has to be embedded in the worldview of the church leaders. Consider the story of Imago Dei.

McKinley didn't set out to find artists for his new church or even to develop an artistic approach to ministry; he set out to reach the unchurched. However, his own personal values included a deep appreciation for the arts. "I'm not an artist," he admits, "but I go to galleries and shows, and I enjoy standing shoulder to shoulder with everyone else." But it wasn't at the galleries where he found his first artistic converts. Those he found in the clubs. McKinley hung out where the music beats its rhythm into the wee hours of the morning and got to know the musicians and their followers. He connected with a few, and, over time, they became involved in Imago Dei. As they got to know their pastor, and as he continued to visit the clubs and galleries and to express his interest in the arts, the musical artists began to invite other artistic friends and acquaintances. It took time, but McKinley's value became the church's value and the arts were woven into everything Imago Dei is a part of.

Many churches believe the answers to attracting artists is to advertise. A quick glance over the "help wanted" bulletin boards at most music stores almost always includes at least a couple of ads for churches searching for musicians to join their church. The answer to attracting musicians and artists is the same as attracting almost anyone to the faith: by building personal relationships with them, not by hanging out a sign reading "Y'all Come!"

Embedding a new value into a church culture isn't an overnight process, and it doesn't happen by inviting a lone artist to do a show once a week. New values come through continuing experiences that result in modified expectations and behaviors. To add art as a value or to add any value to the congregational culture requires leadership's embodiment of that value over a period of time. The more trust the congregation has for the leader, the shorter the period.

Embodying a value is a matter of behavioral change, not dogmatic assertions. The definition of a value is something that's actually important to you, and you can tell what's important to you by evaluating your checkbook and your datebook. You value where you're putting your time and money (Jesus said, "Where your treasure is, there your heart will be also," Matthew 6:21). If you're going to embody art as a value, you'll be spending your resources in the arts. You'll learn to appreciate the subtleties of pointillism and the meter of rap, the shading of cubism and the angst of opera. Not only that, you'll devote time to attending performances and rehearsals. You'll hang out with the actors and the musicians, the sculptors and the taggers. And as your appreciation grows and those relationships build, you'll find opportunities to share your faith journey and listen to theirs. In time, if you're sincere, an artist might walk through your church doors, and perhaps they'll share their talent as an offering of worship.

Or you can take the easier, perhaps more efficient, way. As McKinley suggested, everyone has a creative nature. Within your congregation there are already artists who are willing to share their talents. Some of them are still in school—elementary school. Imagine the joy of a five-year-old who sees his or her Sunday school art used as an illustration in one of the Sunday morning worship PowerPoint slides.[2] Or the excitement of a middle schooler asked to create a digital photo essay for the Sunday stewardship moment on what it means to serve one another. And don't forget the senior adult whose quilts and embroidery on hoops that have stories behind them that could be used to illustrate perseverance, family values, or faithfulness. McKinley has discovered that when you give an artist a space where they can freely express themselves, "you'll get a lot out of them because they want to worship God with it."

That is the point. Imago Dei's strategy for reaching their community is to maximize and use the heartbursts of everyone within the church. Those who have a passion for the homeless work in related missions in the community. Those whose heart beats for those afflicted with AIDS serve alongside local agencies. And those who are artists and express their worship through creativity do so in ministry both inside and outside of the church.

What We Learned

- Arts in the church has to be more than a programmatic add-on. Many church leaders are guilty of attempting to prostitute local artists, from musicians and dancers to painters and actors, in the name of being contemporary or postmodern. Many churches have recently been going out and recruiting artists, often offering compensation, to bring something new and inspiring to their worship services. This has backfired more often than it has succeeded. Worship is a matter of the heart, and when an artist's heart isn't in it, the congregation senses the lack of sincerity. On the other hand, those artists committed to Jesus who are recruited to "do their art" in the worship setting of a church that doesn't embrace art as a value quickly learn that being on display is not conducive to their own spiritual worship, and they usually beat a hasty retreat. However, when a church values, embraces, and encourages artistic expression in worship, artists naturally gravitate to these places and add their gifts to the mix.
- Monasticism is still a viable agenda for the church today. Imago Dei's marriage of art and monastic living in the Artistery is truly inspired and offers an opportunity for young people to become deeply rooted in the faith. Although their monastic experience is limited to one year, this seems to be enough to develop the character, spiritual maturity, and discipline to integrate faith and behavior. It is also clear that there is a growing desire for these kinds of settings in the church today. Imago Dei receives far more applications for the Artistery than they have accommodations. Imagine the effect on the future of Christianity if every community of faith

offered or supported some sort of monastic experience for the young who were still idealistic and energetic enough to dedicate a year or more of their lives to an immersion experience in Christ.

- Numbers aren't how God measures the effectiveness of a church. Ministries like the Artistery probably will never reach large numbers of people, but the people they do reach demonstrate changed lives, which is more than can be said for most people in Christianity today.

- Adding a value to the church's bylaws is vastly different than embedding a value within the culture of a community of faith. Values are what you do more than what you say, and just because a value sounds good doesn't mean that it's going to result in a behavioral change. Many churches say they value evangelism but give neither time nor budget to the process. Few would argue that evangelism is a good thing, but fewer still seem to do anything about it. To embed a new value in the church culture, whether it's valuing the creative arts or evangelism, the church leadership must embody that value long before the community will follow. Stephen George and Arnold Weimerskirch write in *Total Quality Management* that leaders "are under constant surveillance to see whether they will 'break stride.' If they do, people become cynical about the value."[3] New values can only be instilled with an investment in time, behavior, observation, and participation.

- The permission-giving ministry model is timeless. When Peter approached McKinley with the idea of the Artistery, in addition to pledging one hundred dollars a month to the ministry, McKinley gave Peter free reign to develop the ministry without interference as long as it remained within the mission and values of Imago Dei. When a value is embedded in a ministry and that value matches yours, the wise leader allows that ministry to flourish without interference or supervision.

Conclusion

There is a potential for the arts to make a renaissance in the church today, but only if church leaders are willing to embrace the arts as part and parcel of the Christian experience. Today's

American worldview is becoming more and more image and experience based, the two ingredients necessary for an explosion in appreciation of the arts. Church leaders will need to clarify, and perhaps modify, their own values if they are to take the arts seriously in their own contexts.

Response from Rick McKinley, Pastor of Imago Dei

Over the past year we have grown to around 650-700 people. We continue to create space for artists to participate in the life of the community through their gifts. We have brought on Josh Butler as our Creative Arts Director and are able to take a much more intentional approach to reaching the arts community of Portland. From photography exhibits at local coffeehouses to joining with artists from other churches to do community-wide productions, Josh is enabling us to tap more and more of our untapped potential. We have closed down the Artistery because it was unable to make it financially. As a church we poured more and more funds into it, but the ministry itself was not sustainable. It was a great ministry and a great run. We found that the maturity of the people living there was normally not high enough to enter such a structured environment. So, the autonomy of the modern world is alive and well in the urban artists and enforcing the "rules" found to be the bulk of the work that Peter was doing. Peter was growing up as well and got engaged and needed to move on.

Take Two

- God is the ultimate creative artist, but he chose to create us in his image, making us, if you will, apprentice artists. What creative art is buried deep within you that could be offered as an act of worship on your part?
- It's vogue to add art into the church worship service these days. What steps might it take to seamlessly introduce performing and presentation arts into your church worship space without it being forced and fake? What would it look like for art to be such a natural part of your worship that it isn't a programmatic add-on?

- In the parable of the talents in Matthew 25, Jesus had nothing kind to say to the man who hid his talent. Who do you know in your church family who needs to be encouraged to share their talents in worship or in ministry?
- It has been said that you can tell what someone values by looking at their checkbook and their date book. Think about what you consider important in your life. Some common values include health, family, God, and personal growth. Now compare your values with how you spend your money and your time. Are they congruous?
- Now do the same exercise using your church's values, the church calendar, and the annual budget. Does the church need to rethink what it values or how it behaves?

CHAPTER SIX

GREENHOUSE: ORGANIC CHURCH PLANTING

It started as a small network of simple, organic churches called Awakening Chapel. Neil Cole had a vision to start a movement of house churches in North America, similar to the ones in China and India. There, unfettered by denominational rules, congregational polity, or Western church tradition, house churches are multiplying exponentially. Although the actual number of Christians in China is notoriously difficult to discern, it is estimated that 75 percent of them are members of underground, or illegal, house churches.[1] In one region in India, a number of small churches cooperated in starting a house church movement in the midst of an area where 85 percent of the population was Hindu, and the rest of the population primarily Muslim. In five years less than thirty churches had become more than two thousand churches. The only common connection between the churches was a commitment to the Scriptures as the "undisputed authority."[2]

Decentralized networked and nonnetworked house churches make up the majority of the guesstimated ten thousand or so house churches in the United States.[3] These house churches are generally underground or, at least, off most radar screens because they are small and tend to focus on ministry within their immediate community context. Only a few of these house churches advertise their presence beyond their immediate spheres of influence, and fewer still form networks among themselves. However, some house church leaders, such as Neil Cole, have a passion for launching churches that start churches. The resulting daughter and granddaughter house churches will often claim a network through their parentage. Neil Cole's Awakening Chapels are a great example of this organizational structure.

The first Awakening Chapel began in 1998 as an outreach of Church Multiplication Associates (CMA), a group of pastors interested in church planting that was led by Neil Cole. Their first outreach was in a coffeehouse in Long Beach, California. There, the team connected with an urban group of young adults, and within a couple of months, two Awakening Chapel house churches were in operation.

By the end of 1999, there were ten churches in operation with CMA, three of them Awakening Chapels. However, by that time, Neil and CMA had expanded their influence beyond these house churches, and they began to attract Christian leaders from a variety of venues. Many of these were excited about the possibilities of the house church model and, with Neil and his team providing both formal and informal mentoring, house churches began to spring up not only in Californian but also in Arizona, Oregon, and beyond. Many of these new churches claimed their association with Neil and his network, so the counting began. By 2001, there were fifty-three new house churches associated with Neil and his work. In 2002, there were more than one hundred fifty new churches. And by the end of 2003, Neil could account for some four hundred house churches from around the world all claiming some kinship ties to Neil's relational network.

Today, Neil Cole spends much of his time supporting the house church movement in the United States and around the world by offering CMA seminars called *Organic Church Planters' Greenhouse* with his coleader and writer, Paul Kaak. These seminars introduce the house church movement and offer principles and some guidance for launching a house church. From these *Greenhouses*, leaders are raised up and new house churches are launched. These local leaders are encouraged to band together for mutual support and encouragement. When they do, these local networks are considered a part of the larger CMA network of house churches.

The World of House Church

Although the model of house church in America has been getting a good bit of press in recent years and has been touted as a "new wineskin,"[4] the house church is actually the first paradigm used by the newly formed Christian community and, thus, is nearly two thousand years old. These first churches were less about meeting together to "do" church on a weekly basis and more about "being" church. In the early church, families, friends, and neighbors would come together to share a meal and to share life. Their belief system had not yet been splintered out from everyday life, so literally everything they did together was practicing "church." They would eat together and encourage each other in the faith. Whenever a visiting apostle, elder, or traveler from another city would visit, the friends and families would come together to listen and learn. If they were lucky enough to receive a letter, or a copy of a letter, from one of the apostles, again they would gather to hear it read and to discuss it. Church, for the early church, was about a life of faith, not about a meeting.

As the number of Christians grew and as the house churches multiplied, traditions were established within the individual house churches. Meals, worship, teaching, prayer, communion, and collecting alms for the poor were part and parcel of what became weekly house church gatherings.

The planting of multiplying house churches was *the* key to Paul's strategy for reaching the world. For example, although he was only in Thessalonica for two Sabbaths, he managed to start a house church that would become "an example to all the believers in Macedonia and in Achaia" (1 Thessalonians 1:7). Clearly, the house church he planted there multiplied, and, by the fourth century, when the church began to gather in larger gatherings, there were enough Christians to fill the Rotunda, an unused Roman mausoleum.[5]

After Constantine converted to Christianity in 312, he gave the faith legal status and the church began to think and look differently. There were literally thousands of Christians in many of the cities, and they began to look for places to meet together. In 323, at the request of Saint Helen, Constantine's mother, he constructed a building for the church over the site of the nativity in Bethlehem. This structure is generally accepted as the first church building to be constructed for the purpose of Christian worship. Over the next several years, Constantine went on a building spree, constructing church buildings in Rome, Constantinople, and all across Italy. In very short order, church buildings were springing up in every city, town, village, and hamlet.

However, there is some evidence that the age of the house church did not end with the rise of the cathedrals. As Christianity spread through time and space, it regularly experienced persecution. During these troubled times Christianity was regularly pushed out of cities and towns, but at other times and in other places it simply went underground into the homes of the believers.

Indeed, this is the case today in the Middle East, China, India, and parts of Africa. *Wherever the church faces adversity, it turns to its biblical roots and the faithful meet in homes (file this away somewhere).* For instance, when missionaries were expelled from China in 1951, there was great concern in the Western church that all the gains made during the previous decades would be lost. The Chinese government persecuted much of the Chinese church, and, beginning in 1966, there was a concerted effort to eradicate the nation of all religions and the church received even further persecution. However, when the Chinese government readmitted Christian missionaries in the late-1990s, no one was more surprised than those in the West when it was revealed that Christianity had flourished during the previous forty-some years. Today it is estimated that there are somewhere between 75 and 100 million Christians attending house churches across the Chinese nation.[6]

So, what does the world's house church look like today? Mostly it looks busy. Although the Chinese house churches host more than 75 million, most of these are located in the rural provinces. However, there is a concerted effort today to take the house church movement to the Chinese urban population.

The house church in India is also very active today. There are numerous evangelistic efforts going on across the Indian states that are resulting in the planting of thousands of house churches. One small example is a small group of women in India who started forty-seven house churches and baptized 173 people in October 2003.[7]

Other examples abound. In Chile, a single church caught the vision for house church and started seventy-four house churches in one year.[8] From a single evangelistic effort in Ecuador, seventy-five new house churches were started.[9] These are just a few of the cases of the expanding house church movements around the world. The question is, *how well will the house church do in the West?*

Informal Networked and Nonnetworked House Churches

No one knows for sure how the house church networked during the first centuries of Christianity; however, we do know there were connections. In Colossians 4:16, Paul instructs the readers to see that the letter was shared with the church in Laodicea and that the Laodicean letter was read in Colossae. Similarly, in 1 Thessalonians 5:27 he charges the recipient to insure the letter was read to "all of them." Clearly, there was some interchange between the various house churches. Indeed, Paul expected all of his house churches to collect funds for the struggling church in Jerusalem (1 Corinthians 16:1-3).

It seems likely that the early house churches networked together by association. Either their leaders got together occasionally or they kept in contact through letters, getting together as groups, or getting together as individuals. I (BTB) believe that when Paul sent Titus around to the various towns to appoint elders (Titus 1:5), he was doing so in order to more tightly network the local house churches and to put a spiritual parent over them for nurture and direction.

This is one of the chief paradigms used to informally network house churches today. In rural China, spiritual Abbas and Ammas are raised up from within the church to help oversee the house churches.[10] These spiritual parents are responsible for mentoring leaders in the network and for helping to correct errors in belief and practice. They actually have no authority beyond what the house church leaders give them, but in a nation where honor and respect is still valued and practiced, this seems all that is needed.

However, urban Chinese house churches are less networked than their rural brothers and sisters. In the cities, the underground house church is under intense scrutiny. It can be a dangerous thing to be a house church pastor in an unsanctioned church, and the State is constantly trying to find them, infiltrate them, and arrest their leaders. It is common for these house church pastors to be imprisoned for their role in their churches and later released. It is also common for them to return to their house church to continue their work. In any event, because of the fear of infiltration, urban house churches tend to be more independent and less apt to network together. If you don't know about the other house churches, you can't be forced to reveal their location.

The reality is, independent house churches are more the norm than networked house churches. In nations where Christianity is being persecuted, this is understandable. However, there seems to be no really good reason for the independent spirit of the house church in the United States or in other nations where Christianity is free to promulgate its message.

In some cases, pride is at issue. Western house churches are notorious for their prideful attitudes, especially in regard to the established sanctuary-based churches. The we're-right-and-everyone-else-is-unbiblical attitude pervades much of the house church literature. Other house churches maintain their independent spirit because of theological issues. This is more like denominationalism than even the denominations. Many of these house churches in the United States were started because a small group became disenchanted with the sanctuary church and set off on their own to right the wrong. Unfortunately, many of these splinter churches exist primarily for their own comfort rather than to multiply the gospel, so they stew in their own juices and are generally unproductive.

In other cases, the independent spirit is created by ignorance. Because only a minority of house churches have Web sites, or other known connections, they are often unaware of each other, even when in close proximity. Although there are a number of different online options to enhance and make connections with each other, once again, ignorance of these opportunities tends to rule the day.

The key to an effective house church, whether fully networked, informally networked, or nonnetworked, is multiplication. Many house churches, U.S. and otherwise, are stagnant and ingrown because they serve only those within the house itself. It has been said by countless theologians that the church is the only organization that exists for those who are not yet members. The purpose of the church, from the beginning, was to make disciples for Jesus, whether house church or not. A church that does not grow or does not multiply is only fooling itself in thinking that it's a faithful manifestation of the body.

However, multiplication of the church, especially the house church, is meant to be an organic process, as Neil Cole has pointed out. The primary metaphor Jesus used for the church is an agricultural one—vineyards, seed, fruit, harvest, and so on. The key to successful crop farming is in the seed and the cultivation of the soil. Good seed, good cultivation equals a good harvest. Because the quality of the seed reflects the quality and care of the mother plant, it is imperative that a house church pays close attention to its own DNA as it propagates itself. The DNA of the church is the genetic code embedded within it. Things like the mission, the values, the vision, the bedrock beliefs and behaviors all become a part of the very fiber of the church. If a church has good genes, multiplication is more than just expected, it is a reality that simply cannot be thwarted.

Faithful house churches birth new house churches. There is no other alternative. However, in an informally networked system, there is the danger and the concern that wild oats will be scattered in among the domestic oats and a great heresy will emerge. The question is, *what should be done about that?*

According to most house church experts, the answer is nothing, and the Epistles of the New Testament are literally testaments to the resilience of Christianity against "wild oats."

Consider: each epistle written to a church in the New Testament was written to address some problem or another that the church was facing. For instance, the Corinth house church was having a bit of difficulty with their hospitality (1 Corinthians 11). The house church in Thessalonica was troubled with folks who had quit work to await the second coming (2 Thessalonians 3). The Galatian church had been mixing Judaism with Christianity (Galatians 1). All of these were problems that Paul addressed in correspondence as the spiritual Abba.

On the other hand, nonnetworked churches don't tend to have the luxury of oversight. Unless the house church maintains a connection with the mother church (thus making it either a formally or informally networked house church), there are only those within the congregation itself to hold each other accountable and to correct error. This can create an unsavory (at best) and dangerous (at worst) situation within the congregation. Indeed, there have been numerous reports of serious error in many of the nonnetworked Chinese churches. But lest we think heresy is a Chinese-only issue, a variety of errors have popped up in house churches across Africa, Asia, Latin America, and the United States. Indeed, I (BTB) am aware of a local house church where a house church leader has been emotionally abusive and boorishly harsh to his flock, but he justifies it through selective scripture application. Because there is no one in authority to correct him, and he isn't interested in listening to anyone else, the house church plods on ineffective and a poor witness to the love of Jesus Christ.

However (and there always seems to be a however), nonnetworked house churches have been effectively used to spread the gospel, especially in areas of persecution. In China, a house church planter launched a movement of decentralized house churches that has resulted in a number of what are apparently nonnetworked house churches. However, the planter endeavored to implant each church with DNA that emphasized group scripture study and the primacy of scripture for the normative Christian life. By doing so, he maintains that the core teaching will remain, and, in fact, this movement of house churches has multiplied rapidly, nearly tripling in number each year.[11]

Strengths of the Decentralized Organic House Church

Despite the potential issues of a house church without oversight, the fact remains that the majority of house churches in the United States are decentralized and nonnetworked beyond, perhaps, their own mother church. There are a couple of inherent strengths with this paradigm.

First, multiplication of these churches is unfettered by oversight. Networked churches, such as The Rock, provide assessment, teaching, and apprenticeship tools to recruit, train, and launch new house churches (see ch. 7). However, this system, by design, can significantly slow the process of multiplication. Decentralized house churches, although often bereft of formal assessment and training tools, have the ability to raise up leaders quickly and send them out into the harvest. This is one of the clear biblical models demonstrated by Jesus himself. According to Matthew's account, Jesus chose his twelve and almost immediately sent them out to essentially begin church planting (Matthew 10). Arguably, they had virtually no training before they went. Instead they had to rely on the Holy Spirit to lead them. By raising up and sending out leaders from the house church rapidly, it demonstrates that new believers are expected to make disciples from the very beginning. This, of course, is the very time in a new believer's life when he or she is evangelistically most effective, so the notion of rapid multiplication is internalized. We also know from experiencing the church planting movements around the world, including the United States, that all movements rely on rapid deployment of Christians and the planting of new churches.

A second strength of the decentralized house church is that they are infinitely mobile and transplantable. Many are the stories of men, women, and even teenagers who have left their homes to go start house churches in other villages and towns around the world. In the United States, where we're just as likely as not to be living in another state ten years from now, the ability to start a new house church without the red tape of a network can be freeing indeed. And, in fact, it could be one of the most effective ways of reaching our nation. If even a quarter of the Christians who relocated every year started a new house church in their new communities, there would be more than eight million new churches started next year alone.[12]

Weaknesses of the Decentralized Organic House Church

Just as there are strengths in every manifestation of the church, there are also weaknesses. Perhaps the most important weakness of the decentralized house church is the lack of effective accountability. Without some sort of network, there is an inherent risk that each leader will do whatever is right in his or her own eyes, thus leading the house church down a dangerous path. In the past, concerns have been raised about how decentralized churches handle donated funds, the potential for heresy, and the risk of the abuse of power.

A second weakness is the apparent lack of support for decentralized house churches. In Neil Cole's Greenhouse churches, once the house church pastors are trained, they are left with a loose confederation of local house churches that are supposed to meet monthly. However, many of these confederations break down over time and many others don't even get off the ground so the house churches are left with little support. Frankly, there are few resources specifically generated for house church leaders, and so they are left to develop them on their own. There are also few house church coaches or consultants available across the United States to support nonnetworked house churches, and few could afford them even if they wanted to. The issue of financial support may be one of the critical issues of the future for house churches in America.

A third weakness of decentralized house churches is that they have a propensity to be weak and/or ineffective in mission outreach. Scripture exhorts us to "provoke one another" on to good deeds (Hebrews 10:24) and to encourage one another (1 Thessalonians 5). Without encouragement, many house church leaders fold their tents and give up. House churches fluctuate in attendance and even effectiveness just as any other organization does, and when the attendance or effectiveness drops for whatever reasons, there is often no one around to help ward off the discouragement that often surfaces. Similarly, if a house church leader and the congregation receive little ongoing training or support, the potential for growth on multiple levels may be in jeopardy. House churches that don't grow tend to dissipate.

What We Learned

• Informally networked house churches were the biblical norm. It is apparent from even a cursory reading through Paul's letters that the house churches both within a community and across the communities were informally networked. Networks do not necessarily need to be micromanaged in order to remain effective.

- Accountability is key. Although informal networks are the biblical norm, nonnetworked house churches risk error and ineffectiveness by remaining unaccountable to others. Clearly the early house churches were accountable to Paul and later to elders who were appointed across the towns and provinces (Titus 1). House churches in networks that are informally networked seem to remain more focused on multiplication and mission than on focusing on themselves.
- Small multiplies faster and more efficiently than large. Wolfgang Simson, in his book *Houses That Change the World*, turns to nature to compare church multiplication. In the wild, elephants produce a single offspring during a three-year period. On the other hand, rabbits can produce up to 476 million young in a three-year period.[13] The point is, we need more rabbit churches to reach our culture and the world at large.
- Growth and effectiveness are not tied to education. The house church movements in China, India, and around the world depend largely on brand new Christians going out and starting new churches. These new Christians weren't raised in "Christendom," so they don't know the metanarrative of the Scriptures. Instead, they know that Jesus loves them, died for them, rose again, and has set them free. And apparently, in most cases, that's enough to get started. Certainly these new disciples are mentored in the informal networks, but it is clear that growth and effectiveness of the house church movement is more reliant on passion for Jesus than on knowing all the theological tenets of the denomination.
- The faster a group multiplies or the quicker new converts are placed within a cell and involved in ministry the more likely they are to grow in their faith and reach more people. In the United States we tend to spend far too much time training people in classrooms rather than mentoring them in on-the-job ministry.
- Because of the need for networking, we will see the rise of a much more apostolic form of ministry.

Conclusion

Worldwide, the informally networked organic house church is the norm. These house churches tend to reproduce rapidly and have the potential for changing the face of whatever community they plant themselves in. These churches regularly depend on spiritual Ammas and Abbas to oversee them, at least on some level. Although the relationships tend to be voluntary, they are generally strong relationships based on respect. However, the informally networked house churches may not appeal to denominational church planters and church plant supervisors because of the lack of direct accountability. Nonetheless, they remain one of the most vital and viral church models currently on the face of the earth.

Take Two

- The early church met less as a combined congregation and much more as pockets of friends who came together to fellowship, care for each other, wrestle with issues of how to apply what Jesus had taught, and share their combined resources. Today, much of "church life" is about board meetings, committee meetings, team meetings, planning meetings, and so on. Consider, how much time your church is spending to keep the corporate wheels turning? Then consider how much time is spent in developing friendship and kinship groups that spontaneously disciple one another.
- We have stated that the key to an effective house church is multiplication. The same can be said of every form of church. Find out how your church has multiplied itself in the past by starting new churches. Then find out how your church has multiplied small groups like a Sunday school class or a discipleship group. Finally, answer the question, *is it easier to multiply a large corporate church or a small group?* What does this tell you about how to effectively multiply the church?
- The global house church has demonstrated that when Christianity is under persecution, it tends to go underground, and it tends to grow. What kind of adversity do you think is *good* for the church and what kind is *not* good for the church? Is there any way to turn negative adversity into positive results?

CHAPTER SEVEN

THE ROCK HOUSE CHURCH NETWORK: TRAINING, SUPPORT, AND ACCOUNTABILITY

Dropping into The Rock used to be like stepping into any one of a thousand other contemporary churches across America. There was a building, there was a band playing soft pop and Christian rock, and there was a sermon. Because The Rock was founded and grounded in Seattle, you could also get a great latté there, but, outside of that, The Rock looked like "church." But Pastor Bill Tenny-Brittian, a trained and practicing church planter, was somehow uncomfortable. "Seattle has the largest unchurched population in the United States and we weren't reaching them fast enough." So when he heard about a doctoral program that promised to study the worldwide Church Planting Movement, he couldn't resist. And according to Tenny-Brittian, "It ruined me for the traditional church."

Four years and a couple of months after the planting and launch of The Rock Christian Church (Disciples of Christ), Tenny-Brittian cast a vision for a different kind of church—a network of house churches that multiplied rapidly, reached the unchurched, and had money to spare for direct mission. It took nineteen months before The Rock made a successful transition, but transition it did. They sold their building, wrote a detailed strategic plan (think business plan), and moved their base of operations from a single landed location to multiple sites across the Seattle metropolitan area and beyond. Today The Rock is a multiplying house church network with churches in three states and has a "membership" that is significantly greater than when they owned and operated as a more traditionally structured church.

Everything You Always Wanted to Know about House Church but Didn't Know to Ask

"A House Church is the body of Christ that meets in homes. Nothing more and nothing less."[1] But don't let that fool you. A visit to most house churches is nothing like going to "church" in any traditional sense. The gatherings tend to be less structured, *way* less formal, and *way* longer. Gatherings at The Rock are typically two-and-a-half hours long, and often three to three-and-a-half hours. "Sometimes we can't get people to go home," says Tenny-Brittian's wife, Kris. "We've had people in our home until ten or ten-thirty because we're their church and they're comfortable here."

The house church isn't a new movement. The first churches all used homes as their primary meeting places; this became exclusively true after A.D. 70, when the temple in Jerusalem was destroyed and Christianity began to suffer widespread organized persecution. Indeed, the only church structure recognized throughout the New Testament is the house church.

One of the failings of many, if not most, house church proponents is their house-church-only attitudes, at least in their published writings. However, The Rock doesn't see it that way. Tenny-Brittian says,

> We want to be clear that though the only recognized church in the Bible is the house church, we don't for one moment believe that God hasn't used virtually every church structure around the world. There's no question that God has used the great cathedrals, the little white frame buildings, and the open grass huts. We don't think God is concerned about where we meet or how we're structured. If he was, He would have given us a manual like the ones given for the Tabernacle and the Temple.

But Tenny-Brittian adds that the house church is the only model of church that has an instruction manual within the Bible. All the other structures have to adapt and extrapolate.

The house church movement is thriving across the world. David Garrison, a missionary, researcher, and writer for the

International Mission Board of the Southern Baptist Convention, studied church planting movements around the world and notes that house church movements are flourishing in China, India, Cambodia, North Africa, and Latin America. In both China and India, the numbers of house churches have reached into the thousands and thousands. Indeed, in China, one house church movement began with a lone laywoman who launched a church in her home, and in less than ten years this single church has birthed daughter churches, granddaughter churches, and great-granddaughter churches, and so on, until they have reached literally millions of people for Jesus Christ.[2]

But could a house church movement happen in the United States? Certainly. It already has. Centered in Signal Hill, California, Greenhouse can count more than four hundred related house churches.[3] Although the U.S. house church movement cannot yet rival the movements in India or China, a movement is definitely emerging. The Rock House Church Network is one of those that's beneath the radar, but we don't expect it to stay there long.

Doing House Church

Dropping into a house church isn't like going to any other church. Although each house church is unique in how it "does church," there are some common themes.

- Most house churches focus around a meal. Whether it's dinner, lunch, or breakfast, a meal is one of the cornerstones. Perhaps because eating is the most intimate act shared outside of marriage. Eating together fosters and enhances community building. Each house church handles meals differently. Some depend on potluck suppers where everyone brings something. Others depend on the host to cook the lion's share of the meal. And still others rotate the responsibilities. However it's handled, breaking bread together is common around the world.
- House churches tend to be voracious prayer centers. Although virtually every church spends time in prayer, the house church often majors in this practice. Before The Rock transitioned, prayer was a part of everything they did. However, Tenny-Brittian admits that prayer was little more than an add-on in

worship. "We opened, we closed, we offered a few short prayers and one longer prayer during worship, but in total, we probably prayed less than eight or ten minutes in the service." Today, however, most of the house churches we've explored spend significant time in prayer—significant like a half-hour or more in prayer at *every* house church gathering. "When it's a small gathering of the sinners and saints, prayer seems to naturally become one of the most important aspects of what we do."

- Fellowship and caring for one another is the rule, not the exception, in the house church. Because house churches tend to be smaller communities, intimacy develops as a natural by-product of the environment. This intimacy fosters a level of fellowship and caring that is uncommon in churches that aren't small-group dependent. House churches across the board take Acts 4:34 seriously: "There was not a needy person among them." There are more than thirty different "one another"s in the New Testament, "one another"s that pertain specifically to those within the body of believers. House churches generally demonstrate their commitment to one another in how they care for one another. As of this writing, the Seattle Metro community has one of the nation's highest unemployment rates, and this has affected a number of The Rock's house churches. In one of the house churches, the group used their offerings to help a member pay his mortgage when he was between jobs. On another occasion, one of the house churches financially helped support a church-planting pastor from another denomination (and not a house church planter either). The level of fellowship and caring in a house church is unparalleled.

- Virtually every house church emphasizes the study of scripture as a norm. In the more traditional church, Bible study is left for the "Christian Education" department. And though the weekly sermon is often an exposition of a Bible passage, seldom is there any room for discussion between the pastor and the congregation during the delivery—and rarely afterward either. In the house church, however, the weekly "sermon" is most often an open discussion of the Scriptures. These discussions may be free-flowing, or they may be well-structured, but they typically digress to deal with a specific issue the house church or a participant in the house church is facing. Each house church handles the word differently, but the emphasis on the Scriptures is nonetheless a priority in every effective house church.

74

• Almost everything else in a house church is dependent on its own traditions, preferences, and affiliations. Some house churches worship with music and singing; others worship in word and prayer. Some take up a weekly offering; others receive offerings only when there's a need. Some celebrate communion regularly; others seldom share the bread and cup. The four common themes are nearly universally practiced. Everything else in a house church is fluid.

The Rock House Church Network

During the nineteen months between vision-casting and implementation of The Rock House Church Network, Tenny-Brittian spent his time studying the house church movement, experimenting with form and structure, and putting together a strategic plan that focused on multiplication of disciples, leaders, and churches. Because he was a part of the Christian Church (Disciples of Christ), he had the latitude to experiment and innovate; however, as he put together his plan, he held in tension the need for flexibility in the house church against the need for accountability to the DNA of the network. The result was the wedding of structure with spontaneity through training, support, and accountability.

House Church Training

One can't explore The Rock's Web site (www.therockcc.us) without noticing the emphasis on discipleship and leadership training. "Training begins from your first visit to the house church," says Tenny-Brittian. Every week, the network produces a Bible study called *Blueprints* that focuses on discipleship training within a house church model. The house churches in the network are not required to use or follow the *Blueprints* study, "but we want to make it inconvenient *not* to." The various house churches occasionally use other studies within their own congregations. The *Alpha Course, Forty Days of Purpose*, and book studies on *Mere Christianity* have been used across the network churches. The network depends on the house church pastors to recognize and address the needs of their congregations, so they need the flexibility to teach as the Holy Spirit leads.

75

Other discipleship training materials include the *Foundations* Bible study, a six-week study used during the first six weeks of a new house church launch. These materials introduce the new house church participants to the historical house church and the five purposes of the church by studying selected scripture passages. The first *Foundations* session begins with a video introduction that walks the participants through Bible study. Once a core group in a new house church finishes *Foundations*, they have been exposed not only to how a house church functions but also to what is expected of a disciple of Jesus Christ according to the Scriptures.

The identification, recruiting, and training of leaders is a core practice of The Rock. House church pastors are trained from the beginning to identify potential leaders of future house churches through observation and tools available to them through the network. During the first few weeks of a participant dropping in to a house church, they are invited to go online and take the Personal Ministry Assessment (PMA). The PMA is a series of inventories that helps participants identify their spiritual gifts, their personality profile, their leadership preference, and their ministry passions. Once they've taken the inventories, the network scores them and assembles a presentation that is sent to the house church pastor. The pastor then schedules a session with the participant to go over their PMA. Leaders of future house churches are often identified during this process, and the house church pastor is trained to encourage the participant to consider this calling.

Most of the current house church pastors in The Rock Network have been recruited from existing and newly launched house churches. According to Tenny-Brittian, "It seems that one of the best times for us to look for leaders of future house churches is within the first six weeks. They're excited, they're motivated, and they're ready to do something significant for the Lord."

Training of future house church pastors begins as they are apprenticed within their own house churches. The apprenticeship program of The Rock House Church Network is less than methodical but seems to be effective nonetheless. Because leadership in a network church is shared, an apprentice can expect to experience and lead every facet of a house church gathering during their training. Several times each year, the network offers House Church Pastor Training Seminars that introduce and train prospective house church pastors in the basics of leading a house church within the network structure. Once the training is complete, the apprentices are invited to enter into a covenantal relationship with the network, and, for those who do, a countdown commences toward the launching of a new house church.

Once a new house church is launched, network training continues. Monthly mentoring appointments with each house church pastor ensures that leadership is trained in new skills as they are needed. Additionally, there are leadership seminars three times a year and a seven-year course of study that allows the house church pastor to experience the rigors of seminary level courses without the expense or the full-time commitment to a graduate program.[4] For leaders in The Rock House Church Network who are gifted and called to full-time ministry, there are several other Training Modules that prepare them to serve within The Rock's structure in salaried leadership positions.

Training at The Rock is both extensive and ongoing. The materials are written in-house and are specifically slanted for use in a networked house church system. These materials are being prepared by the network for licensing and distribution to other house church networks.

House Church Support

Anyone who has been in a pastorate for a couple of years has stories about feeling "alone" in the midst of their congregations and denominations. Imagine the feelings of isolation you might get if you were the pastor of a church that wasn't recognized as a legitimate congregation by the majority of church leaders. Such is the life of many, if not most, house church pastors. However, at The Rock, the house church pastors have a network of support they can rely on.

Support at The Rock begins with the weekly Bible Leaders' Discussion Groups (BLDG). This is a weekly gathering of local house church pastors who come together to go over the *Blueprints* Bible study, exchange offering envelopes for fresh ones, and take the time to support each other with their prayers, experience, and insights. The BLDG program is also an opportunity for the house church pastors to take the time to worship together. Every house church pastor is expected to attend one of the weekly BLDG programs. However, there are some house church pastors who don't live within driving distance to the Seattle-based network. For these, a webcam and computer hookup has been a godsend as the house church pastors make long distance connections with their colleagues.

The Rock also provides one-on-one mentoring for all the house church pastors and all the apprentices. Trained mentors with house church experience work through a variety of issues with their house church pastor mentorees including building character, improving their ministry skills, and exploring the multiplication of disciples, leaders, and churches. These mentoring relationships offer significant support to the house church pastors because of the relationships that are established and nurtured over time.

Besides the personal support offered to the house church pastors, The Rock House Church Network provides a wealth of material support for the house church and their pastors. The network has produced recruiting videos for use by house church participants to help them invite their unchurched friends and neighbors to their house church. The Web site has also been designed to support the house church and their pastors by serving as a recruiting tool as well as providing support by way of training articles, news, and most of the training materials used in the various seminars.

The Rock House Church Network is committed to ensuring that its leadership knows they are there for them. They try to make this clear through their training classes and in every communication they provide.

Accountability

According to Tenny-Brittian, accountability is one of the chief stumbling blocks that falls before denominational leaders when the subject of house church comes up. Everyone wants to know how to control the house church, especially how to "keep it line" with denominational practices. "The reality is, you can't *control* any church. Some denominations are allowed to fire or remove the pastor. Some are allowed to close the building to the church folks. And most can withhold support. But you can't control a church. Like Gamaliel said to the Sanhedrin: If it's of God you can't stop it. If it's not, you won't have to."

Nonetheless, The Rock seems to hold some reins tightly. For one, they expect their leaders to be in an accountability group. Participation in these groups requires daily Bible reading, prayer, and a weekly face-to-face where a litany of accountability questions are asked. The Rock also requires their leaders to attend the weekly BLDG program where the state of the individual house churches are discussed openly.

The capstone of a house church's accountability is the House Church Pastor's Covenant that is required of every leader. Subscription to the covenant means that every leader agrees to support the vision, mission, values, beliefs, and behaviors of The Rock. Leaders also agree to practice the spiritual disciplines, especially the accountability partnership, as well as to attend and participate in the training events offered by the network. In return, The Rock agrees to continue to support and train the leaders on a number of levels including recruiting, launching, and providing appropriate materials for the house churches.

The question of accountability, in terms of keeping the house churches "under control" seems to be moot. Tenny-Brittian says,

> If a church or a church leader steps outside of our bedrock behaviors or the covenants, we practice Matthew 18. If they don't turn it around, we really only have one option and that's to withdraw our support. We can't close them and since most of the time the church meets at the pastor's house, it's pretty difficult to remove the pastor. So we just stop supporting and including them.

The Rock expects to lose as many as 10 percent of their house churches every four years, but according to Tenny-Brittian, most of the ones that close will do so because of the transience of our society. Today, families move as often as every seven years, so some house churches close simply because leadership relocates. Sometimes, however, this gives The Rock an opportunity to open new house churches in new locations. "We have people moving all the time, and many of the folks who've been in a house church for some time simply don't want to go back to a more traditional church. So we offer to train them and then support them from afar," says Tenny-Brittian.

Accountability is one of the core values of The Rock, and it is built into the structure of the church in virtually every aspect. But as accountable as the leaders and churches are, it all comes down to trust. "We have to trust our leaders. We pray about it, we recruit and enlist them, we train them, and we offer our ongoing support. Then it's up to them."

Conclusion

House church networks are springing up all over the world. From India to Indiana, rapidly multiplying networks are being established and are changing communities. However, few of these networks receive significant support from one house church to another. Most of the house church networks appear to be launching sites, but there is little if any accountability, training, or support structures beyond the first or second generation of church starts. Some have expressed concern about this, especially in China, where reportedly aberrant pockets of churches are emerging within some of the house church movements. It might be well to remember that Paul had some of the same issues when he started house church networks across Asia Minor. Occasionally, he had little time to establish the DNA of Christianity within the community. He only had two Sabbaths in Thessalonica before he had to flee, and yet he left a church network that became one of his flagship churches (1 Thessalonians 1:7). Indeed, he had to send Titus back to a number of his house churches to raise up leaders in his absence (Titus 1:5). Even so, every one of Paul's letters combated some sort of heresy that was plaguing the newly formed churches. Why would we think we would be any different? The Rock certainly seems poised to deal with the issues as they arise, but as they say, some churches are simply going to move on.

The writer of Ecclesiastes asserted that there is a time for every season, and perhaps the season is right for a new crop of house churches. Every survey, study, or article written on the emerging generations refers to their distrust of institutional religion and their disdain for their lack of intimacy. Seeing the potential of the House Church Movement should be a no-brainer.

Only time will tell if these networks receive the sponsorship and get the nod from denominational leaders. If so, we may see mainline churches dotting every community in America once again.

What We Learned

- The fear that networking and accountability will stifle the effectiveness of the House Church Movement may well be unfounded, at least in the North American context. Although time will be the final judge, The Rock seems to be multiplying at the expected rate of one new house church per existing church each year.
- Simple church, as house church is sometimes referred to, can be a misnomer in a network of house churches. Although each house church itself runs quite simply with a lay pastor and a small flock encouraging one another in the faith, a network of house churches is another matter. Just like any organization—or organism for that matter—the structure of a house church network can seem complex. Because The Rock provides ongoing training, support, and accountability structures for its house church pastors, it has developed a system of feedback and checks and balances to ensure no one is left behind and no one is left alone.
- Networked house churches close, just like other churches. People move and leaders lose interest and resign to leave the House Church Movement. However, because the majority of the house churches continue to reproduce, the loss of a single house church is less traumatic. Indeed, in some cases it means that there are new leaders who have suddenly become available to start something new.

Take Two

- Church leaders, whether of the lay type or clergy type, need ongoing training and support. Take a look at your church's training program and discuss how it is preparing leaders to serve.
- Accountability in the church is often a matter of holding the pastor accountable for virtually everything that goes on in a church. Consider and discuss how your church holds its volunteer leaders accountable. Does your congregation remove someone who is not doing the job, or does it allow them to continue in order to be "nice"? How could your church change this?

- Virtually every church in the United States has a variety of small groups, whether they are home groups, Sunday school groups, choir groups, or board groups. How are your small groups reflecting Jesus? How are they reaching out to others? How are they reaching in to encourage themselves? And, most important, how are they multiplying?

CHAPTER EIGHT

ZERO-BASED MINISTRY: TAKING MINISTRY TO THE STREETS

Because of the nature of this form of emerging ministry, we felt it best to share two examples of what we are calling zero-based ministry.

The Rock Community Church (UMC)

Walking into the area around the Tyler Apartment Complex is like walking into another world. It might help you get a picture of what the area looks like to know that the complex is the oldest privately owned government-funded housing project in Tennessee. Being privately owned means it has fewer rules to follow, which usually means the housing project is far more run-down than other publicly operated projects. (It is run-down due to being the oldest in the state.) It is fair to say that the area is one of the poorest areas in Johnson City, Tennessee. To make matters worse, the area borders the Johnson City Country Club, separated only by chain-link fence. A person can stand in the apartment complex and see the golfers with their GPS golf carts. "This is one of the biggest contradictions I've seen in my life," says Randy Hensley, Executive Director of Coalition for Kids and pastor of The Rock Fellowship United Methodist Church. "The [golf] carts cost $1,200, and some of the mothers [of the housing project] sell the new clothes or toys we give their kids to get drugs. The wealthiest and the poorest—side by side with no connection."

In the early 1990s a small United Methodist church near the complex was considering installing a fence to separate itself from the unsightly low-rental complex. Instead, a new pastor entered the scene and motivated the church to begin a ministry to the children of the area. They began with a playground and a big dream with no idea how to pull it off, much less the personnel to accomplish it. Enter 1998 and Randy Hensley. Randy was the pastor of a rural congregation that he had seen grow from a handful of people into a thriving country church. By sheer happenstance the pastor of the small Methodist church crossed paths with Randy and offered him the job of starting this ministry to disenfranchised kids. After turning them down several times, Randy finally agreed to lead the project while remaining at his church. "We didn't do any research. We just saw the kids; saw the need; and it happened. It's a God thing. You don't raise $500,000 in less than a year unless it is a God thing. It's all about God." Although the small Methodist church pastor had seen the need and recruited Randy, he released the ministry to Randy and a board of directors.

And indeed it seems like it must have been truly a God thing. Without any major financial backing, except for one individual with a strong financial commitment to helping the ministry succeed, Randy began the Coalition for Kids, a 501(c)(3) in 1999 with a budget of $180,000 and two staff members. Today the organization has a staff of twenty and a budget of $360,000. The financial support comes mostly from private donations, but recently Coalition for Kids was picked up by United Way, the first addition to the community charity in that area in twenty years.

Coalition for Kids is a ministry to at-risk kids, grades one through seven, which has grown from existing for the apartment complex of Tyler to a Washington County–wide program. In the summer the ministry runs every day from 7:30 to 5:00, including meals, Bible study, field trips, and recreation. During the school year the ministry runs an after-school program until 8:00 P.M. that includes a tutoring program that students can enter only by a referral from someone at their school. The tutoring ministry is so popular it is now being done at five sites: the Community Center, which houses the Coalition for Kids, a Baptist church, a Christian church, a school, and a Hispanic ministry in an apartment rented by a partnering Presbyterian church. The apartment is in the Hispanic community.

As the ministry grew, so did the drain on Hensley. Two things bothered him: having to pastor a church at a distance while running this growing, new organization and the fact that he knew the Coalition for Kids was doing five days a week what the church should be doing anyway. The only thing missing was a worship service.

During the summer of 2001, Randy left the rural church he was pastoring to start The Rock Fellowship Church in the metal building that houses the Coalition for Kids (only a hundred yards from the Methodist church where it all began). When I (BE) asked Randy why he really started the church, the passion in his voice intensified.

> I saw a lot of unchurched people, mostly lower income, who weren't going to church because either they didn't feel they were good enough or they felt as if they had to dress up to go to church. There are a lot of churches that have buses that pick up the kids, save them, and then leave them alone. So we started a church where these folks don't have to dress up and can have a sense of ownership and respect because they are looked at as equal, not handouts. The disenfranchised need someone to talk to. They don't expect you to fix their world; they just want to talk about their world.

In Randy's words, "We're a come-as-you-are church. Raw religion—we preach, we sing, and we leave. No flash. There have been some bizarre experiences."

By most congregations' standards, many of the things that happen around The Rock do seem crazy. It is not uncommon in worship for Randy to have to call down a youth or have an adult talk back while in a sermon. Often he walks the isles during worship and, while preaching, asks youth to quiet down, turn around, and face forward. One Sunday, a lady lit a cigarette in the middle of the service. After about two draws, she realized what she was doing and got up and left. On another Sunday, an eight-year-old boy asked the congregation to pray for his mom, who had been missing for two months. Later, Hensley found out that the boy's mom was in jail and had given her kids to a relative to prevent Children's Services from taking the child and his four siblings. Another Sunday, a young woman told the church, "I want to praise God because I just got my second negative AIDS test." One Sunday, a kid stole a car, picked up four girls, and came to church. After church, the man who owned the car appeared. He called the police, but by the time they arrived, the man decided to give the boy a second chance. There's a realness to these folks and their worship that you don't often find in a more typical congregation. They're just-who-they-are kind of people, people who are who they are and don't feel the need to cover up the truth or posture themselves. What you see is what you get.

The worshiping congregation of around one hundred is unusual. Around 40 percent are youth and children (many of whom come from the Coalition for Kids), there's one wealthy family, six or seven people over fifty, and another third are college students, most of whom are in some form of mission.

South Street Ministries

It happened every afternoon one summer at four o'clock on West South Street in Akron, Ohio. Men gathered, held hands and prayed, and then walked the streets of South Akron wearing caps and blue jackets designed with an outline of a city, a cross, a handshake, and the words "SEEK THE WELFARE OF THE CITY—JEREMIAH 29:7." As they walked down the streets, they stopped to talk to the kids, calling them by name; store owners welcomed them with pride; and ailing residents relished their visit. The men in blue gave meaning once again to the word *neighborhood*.

Duane Crabbs, pastor of the South Street Ministries, organized the street chaplaincy in 1997 in response to the second slaying of a Palestinian convenience store owner in six months. This street is just one of many ways South Street Ministries has responded to the needs of the area. "Our ministry is about being in the neighborhood; we want to be good neighbors," Duane says. "We don't want to be like other ministries that come in and leave to go back to their own communities. We're present 24-7."

The bottom line for South Street Ministries is to develop relationships in the neighborhood. "A lot of what I do is being available to people. I try to hear people where they're at and connect them to Christ. I came here thinking I could fix a neighborhood. I couldn't. Now I try to help people stay connected to Jesus Christ in the midst of their brokenness."

Duane and Lisa Crabbs struggled for four years over what God was calling them to do. Duane was a paramedic in the Akron, Ohio, fire department, happily married, and making good money. Together, they owned a very nice house and were blessed with four children, seventeen and younger. But something was missing.

In 1997, they felt called to south Akron to a poor, transient, crime-ridden neighborhood. The sign over a local bar sums up the neighborhood: "Your first fight here will be your last fight here." When describing his passion for the South Street area Duane said, "There are fourteen bars and fourteen churches in this area. The problem is the bars are open seven days a week and the churches aren't. We've at least changed that."

Duane and Lisa felt that they were called not to "minister" to the neighborhood but to be neighbors in the name of Christ. They felt that meant a twenty-year commitment to live in the neighborhood. They found a large condemned house sitting on an acre of land (an amazing thing in that neighborhood) and began being a neighbor. The essence of South Street Ministries isn't as much in what it does as in who it is: neighbors to those on the margins who usually don't have neighbors.

One story best describes the essence of South Street Ministries. One day during the early years, a very large black man named Patrick came up to Duane and asked him why he was always trying to help people. When Duane explained he was on a mission from God to be neighbor to the people of South Street, the man asked him if was willing to go "where the good shepherd doesn't often go looking for his sheep." Duane said he would and got in the car with the man who took him to a private bar. Duane was the only white man in the room. They ordered a drink and then Patrick got up and left Duane all alone. Soon another man came over and sat down and started talking to Duane about the explicit sex acts he had done. Duane became very uncomfortable. The man left to go to the restroom and Patrick came back. "How's it going?" he asked. Duane replied, "I'm uncomfortable." Patrick played it down. Duane continued. "No man, I'm really, really uncomfortable. Can we leave?" "No. If you leave here now they will smell the fear on your face forever." With that, Patrick left Duane alone again and the man came back from the restroom and the explicit conversation began again.

In time the man left at which point Patrick returned. "Well Duane, you did good. We can go now," Patrick said.

"Why did you bring me down here?" asked Duane. "To mess with me?" Patrick looked at him and asked, "Why do you think people come to this bar?" "To get drunk?" Duane replied. "Not so. They come for fellowship," Patrick explained.

Continuing, Patrick pointed to the bartender and said, "You see that bartender? He's heard more confessions than a priest. You know how uncomfortable you feel in here? Well that's how these folks feel when they come to your place. If you're going to do ministry here you've got to get comfortable on their turf!" Patrick's visit was a turning point in Duane's ministry.

Duane resisted becoming a "church" for over five years because he did not feel it was his calling at the time. Instead, they started Scouting programs for boys in the neighborhood. Then a bike club where they teach the kids how to rehab bikes and then take bike hikes. They converted the second story of their garage into a youth center. They held weekly Bible study and prayer sessions for forty to fifty people in their living room while the children were cared for by folks from a friend's church. Duane became a fabulous teacher of the Bible even though he's never been to college or seminary. Listening to Duane is like listening to a mixture of evangelical Campus Crusade and Sojourner's social justice.

The ministry on South Street has been at best difficult and at worst life draining. "If you're not on guard, this neighborhood will drain the life out of you," Duane confided. But still they stay and try to be the good Samaritan we have all read about but seldom met.

Bring It Home

Randy Hensley and Duane Crabbs are pastors of what we call a zero-based church. A zero-based church is a church that initially began as a ministry and only later developed into a church.

We believe the further we go into the twenty-first century we will see a growing number of zero-based congregations. Zero-based ministries have been around a long time. However, we feel they could be a major player in the emerging world. The times are ripe for the expansion of this form of ministry. The post-Christian crowd will be much more reluctant to pay for big buildings. Fewer leaders will go to seminary and still want to do ministry.

Zero-based Christian leaders don't focus on the growth of an institutional church. Instead, they focus on transforming individuals and changing the countryside, village, town, or city, and yes, even the world. Their goal is never about a building or saving a church.

We don't think many established church leaders get this distinction. IT'S NEVER ABOUT BUILDING A CHURCH; IT'S ALWAYS ABOUT CHANGING A PEOPLE GROUP OR AN AREA OR CITY. Building a church focuses leaders inward on a small group of people. Changing a people group or area focuses leaders outside the walls of the church. As John Wesley said, "The world is my parish." If more of us would begin thinking and preaching this way, more of us would spend more time in the community than we do in our church. We hope this distinction catches on.[1]

The passion of these leaders has shifted from the old traditional models to new paradigms of vision.

- From building a church to reaching an area through multiple types of partnerships;
- From thinking inward to thinking outward so that the primary focus of time, energy, and money is on those in the area or world who do not yet know Jesus Christ.
- From saving an institution to saving a region, which requires a focus on mission rather than theology and partnership rather than exclusive and competitive ministries.
- From being just a pastor to functioning as a missionary or even an apostle;
- From building walls and fences to keep out the riffraff to erecting bridges between differing microcultures and people groups, even (especially!) bridges between the saved and the unsaved;
- From expecting people to "come grow with us" to fulfilling the biblical mandate to go and witness in Jerusalem, Judea, Samaria, and the ends of the world;

• From doing programs that people attend to nurturing communities where people grow;
• From resources provided by the denomination to resources birthed in effective congregations;
• From searching for people with seminary credentials to preferring people with demonstrated credentials;
• From focusing on institutional size to developing a passion for the size of the kingdom.

Response from Randy Hensley, Pastor of The Rock Fellowship Church

As I look at ministry today I am more concerned that the church has lost its passion and, therefore, works in futility, for no one follows anything without passion. The reason the ministry we are involved in has worked is that there is a true desire (passion) to impact the lives of those less fortunate. When we stand up for those who cannot stand for themselves, God honors that servant attitude. He also sends those who have resources to those who have need and have shown responsibility. We are in the change-a-life business, we believe that getting too concerned over how big the program is can take away from what the church was intended to be: a setting where everyone is someone and where all deserve to be treated as someone while treating others the same. The church for too long has given so much "stuff" and money that it has forgotten that most people, if given respect, would have more than money could buy.

As I see the church today, it stands afraid of the world, afraid the world will infiltrate and bring dishonor to God through them. It stands shaking as if we need to be building barricades to protect ourselves. It seems to be more concerned about its own neck than the souls of the lost in a world that teaches "take care of yourself." From that perspective the church itself looks a little like the world with its worry-about-me attitude, and that will draw no one into the freedom and victory God offers. We have got to become a servant body again, where people are taught that they are to consider others higher than themselves no matter how much they serve or give—not servant leaders, but servants. The church is so like the world that it will not let go of the title *leader*, almost as if it is afraid the people will leave if they aren't patted and praised enough.

This is a dirty job, it has very little rewards, it can get ugly, and it can turn your stomach, but it is the right thing to do! I believe when the church truly gets personal with the world, whether rich or poor, it will find such a degree of hurt and pain and dispair that only the passionate will survive and sense the God that can overcome and change lives.

May this book take those people and give them hope for their dreams and joy for their soul, and in the process, build up the body of Christ.

What We Have Learned

- You don't have to have a church building or even a congregation to do ministry. Institutional worship doesn't have to be the foundation of a Christian ministry. In fact, most biblical ministry was done without a church. Maybe it's time we got back to the basics: working with people rather than institutions.
- A leader is always a leader in the right environment. Both Randy and Duane are down-to-earth people just like the areas that they serve.
- Instead of thinking about how to get people out of their seats and into the streets, these ministries have realized that effective ministry often takes leaders from the streets to the seats. Ministry today requires more of a "go" mentality than the old come-worship or grow-with-us mentality. These ministries prove the importance of a missional mind-set.
- Our biggest worry about zero-based churches is their funding. It seems that the leader has to spend enormous amounts of energy just finding enough money to survive, and getting into bed with the government and their "faith-based funding grants" has eroded the effectiveness and evangelistic zeal of several worthwhile Christian ministries.

Take Two

- What changes would you have to make for the distinction between reaching an area for Christ and building a church to be evident in your actions and those of your congregation?

- Evaluate how you spend your time and for whom the programs in your church are designed. Is the focus more on the existing church and its members than on the surrounding area or world? What would you have to do to make the focus more on being a witness to those not yet connected to Jesus?
- What do you value the most: the place where you worship or the fulfillment of the Great Commission? When you think *church* do you see people or a building?
- Perhaps there is a zero-based church in your area. Why not put them in your budget?
- You can find The Rock Community Church and Coalition for Kids at www.coalitionforkids.org/.
- South Street Ministries doesn't have a Web site. As Duane said, "that's not our clientele." Consider what you and your church do that may not be reaching your clientele.

CHAPTER NINE

WHY SOME UNDER-THE-RADAR CHURCHES WILL GO THE WAY OF THE WIND

Since we began writing *Under the Radar* a number of churches we had considered for this project have ceased to exist or had transitioned into something less than they had envisioned. For instance, one cell-based church had an exciting monthly gathering that they had hoped would become a focal point. The gathering has since ceased and the multicelled church is down to one home group that hasn't done much for more than a year. In another case, a church was using an arts and media model that looked promising. It incorporated a three-week study of a biblical theme using one week for Bible study, a second week for arts expression, a third week for a media presentation and discussion, followed by a fourth-week worship service that melded the three weeks' contributions into a circle gathering. This too, however, has passed by the wayside and was disbanded. And these are only two of many we are aware of that have down-sized, adopted a new or more traditional model, or ceased to exist.

We've looked at these churches and taken the temperature of our culture in order to offer these insights. We honestly don't expect all of the churches we've written about to exist in another ten years. We hope they do, but, the fact is, these are great experiments and new untried models that have been launched in a hostile environment. Some of them, unfortunate as it may seem, are going to cease to exist. Following are some of the problems that, we believe, will cause the demise of some of the churches.

Lack of Evangelistic Zeal

Possibly one of the most disturbing findings we've experienced is that many of the new models simply do not place a high value on evangelism. Indeed, I (Bill T-B) had a conversation with a layperson while attending an emerging church (one that no longer exists, incidentally), and I asked him about how the church reached non-Christians and the unchurched. His response was, "Oh, we don't really do that. We might invite a friend or two sometimes, but we're not about evangelism." Lest you think this was simply a misinformed individual, I later spoke with the pastor, who echoed the same sentiments.

And this is not an isolated case. We have spoken with a number of emerging church pastors and participants who share a similar view. The fact is, in many of these churches evangelism is simply not on *their* radar screens.

The issue seems to be, in some of the under-the-radar emerging churches, that there is an underlying distaste for large, "impersonal," institutional churches. So when a small group of folks get together to start a new church with a new paradigm, they invite their friends, launch a church, and nestle in and get comfortable. But then they almost immediately stop trying to reach others lest they destabilize their intimate community and become too large. As much as the church's leadership might admire the ministries of Mars Hill in Seattle or the Bay Area Fellowship in Corpus Christi, Texas, they are afraid of becoming too bureaucratic or so large that they lose the intimacy of relationships they so desire.

This particular dilemma is certainly not unique to emerging churches. Indeed, this is the very reason most U.S. churches are sinking slowly into the setting sun. It comes down to comfortability. When we build a small group of close-knit friends, it is difficult to bring in someone from the outside. When we do, it messes up the group dynamics something terrible, and so we often unintentionally "close" our groups after a couple of months and subtly do everything we can to maintain the status quo.

To make matters worse, some of these churches aren't really sure why they *should* be reaching out to others. In the Western

94

world there is a pervading attitude of live and let live. When it comes to our faith walks, this is generally translated as "you believe like you want and I'll believe like I want" with an unspoken agreement that "if you don't try to convert me, I won't try to convert you." However Jesus didn't give us an option about who he was in relationship to the rest of the world, and he didn't give us a choice about whether or not evangelism was an optional part of *his* plan. Evangelism is the prime directive of a biblical church and every faithful disciple!

Lack of Gifted, Entrepreneurial Leadership

In the early days of American Christianity, gifted and entrepreneurial individuals regularly mounted horses and set out to start churches across the frontier. These rugged individuals would ride onto homesteads and into the small towns springing up across the continent, gather a small crowd and start a worshiping body. Then over the months they would ride a circuit between these small churches and bring the word of God from congregation to congregation. As the churches grew, they would either raise up their own leaders or the circuit-riding preacher would enlist someone in the congregation or bring someone in from the outside and the process would continue.

Fast forward to the twentieth century and we find these rugged, entrepreneurial church planters replaced by well-trained seminary graduates whose model of ministry is chaplaincy and pastoral care. Now, there's not a thing wrong with these wonderfully devoted purveyors of ministry, but today when we look around, most of the entrepreneurial leaders are busy starting dotcoms and selling Morris Minis or securities. They are *not* out starting churches, and very few entrepreneurial church planters are found in our seminaries.

This is exacerbated by the sociological reality that like attracts like. If you take a personality temperature of churchgoers across America, you will discover that the vast majority of our faithful memberships have gentle and pastoral spirits, much like the pastors who have led their churches for decades. And those individuals who are exciting and spiritually gung ho have been more tolerated than embraced by the church—they sort of stand out as the aberration. And because the majority of our spiritual leaders of tomorrow come from these congregations, our seminaries are filled with gentle ministers rather than innovative entrepreneurs.

This means that our best-trained church leaders are generally ill-suited to start new churches because it can be exceedingly difficult to gather a crowd if your personality and training are better matched for reflective listening rather than persuasive inviting. And yet, a few graduating from our seminaries, and many more in our churches, are dissatisfied with church business as usual and they want to do something about it. And since it is infinitely more difficult to remodel an existing structure, and virtually impossible to change an existing church, these individuals are setting out to start new churches.

Which brings us back to the problem. These warm-hearted individuals set out to start something new and they gather a few like-minded friends—friends who are generally unhappy with the church's status quo—and they launch a new church. But without an entrepreneur to spearhead the effort, without a person-magnet, these efforts regularly fail to achieve what is called critical mass, that is, enough people to financially support the effort or to sustain the necessary energy to grow beyond themselves over time. When critical mass isn't achieved, most new churches die on the vine; indeed, as many as 80 percent of all new church starts cease to exist within a couple of years, most because they did not achieve sustainability. And without charismatic leadership, it is difficult to gather the necessary crowd.

Several of the emerging churches we visited were being led by sincere, wonderful men and women whose hearts were to be faithful to the Great Commission by starting new churches. However, these same pastors were often introverted, pastoral-care driven, and having significant difficulty in gathering a crowd. Without a sustaining congregation, most of these emerging churches will cease to exist in a short time; indeed, at least one of the congregations we visited has already disbanded for this very reason.

Lack of Thinking Ahead

Most church-planting boot camps require significant planning, but that hasn't stopped the unplanned launching of new church models by both trained and untrained church leaders. The word *planning* has taken on negative connotations and images such as "corporate" or "business" model or "in-the-box" thinking. Some church leaders complain that the notion of planning stifles the movement of the Holy Spirit. Planning, and especially *strategic* planning, seems almost to be a dead art in corners of the emerging church world.

We prefer to talk about strategic mapping. Mapping is simply a rough topographical look at where you are compared to where you want to be; it then suggests a route to get there. We all know that along the route their will be detours and false trails and some backtracking. Strategic mapping is meant to be a guideline, not a heartless dictum.[1]

Of the models we looked at for this book, several were quite plan-oriented. The Rock House Church Network has a five-year strategic plan that projects income, expenses, and development milestones. On the other hand, many of the churches we have looked at have little more than a vague idea of where they're going or how they're going to get there.

There is a wonderful *Peanuts* comic strip that shows Charlie Brown shooting arrows at a fence and then walking up to the fence and painting targets around each arrow—an easy way to hit the bull's-eye. This is a metaphor for many of our churches today: they don't know where they're going, but when they get there they're sure they're going to hit the center of the target.

The fact is, planting any church is plain hard work, and planting a new emerging church is harder still since there are few marked trails to follow. Someone said that Jesus never said being obedient to the Great Commission was going to be easy; he just said it was all going to be worth it. If church leaders are going to plant effective churches that will reach the unchurched, they are going to have to take on the task of deciding what it is they believe God is trying to achieve through their ministry and then prayerfully map out what it will take to get there. There are many different ways to write an effective strategic map, including the adaptation of business software to suit the situation, but, in our experience, virtually *any* thoughtful and thorough mapping in advance is well worth the time. There is little worse than having to deal with significant issues that crop up at the last minute that could easily have been avoided if just a little planning had been undertaken in advance.

Lack of Financial Planning

Although this is related to strategic mapping, financial planning warrants a mention of its own. We have no idea how many churches we've watched fold their tents because the founding pastor couldn't survive financially, but the numbers are staggering. Many good-hearted church leaders jump out of the safety of either their religious or secular jobs to launch a new venture and have no real idea of the sacrifice that is required of them. Six months to a year later they realize that they simply can't survive on what their new church can afford to give (often little to nothing) and with heartbreaking discouragement they close the doors on their "baby."

Both of us believe that ministry is a calling, not a career. Fred Craddock warned his preaching classes that "contrary to popular opinion, Jesus did not die on the cross so that preachers could make a living." If you haven't counted the cost, don't pick up the cross. Church planting is a labor of love and the age of denominations writing huge checks to start new congregations is largely over. Today we are aware of denominations that regularly offer their new church planters as little as $3,000 per year to help finance a new church start. If you are called to start a church, financial planning is a must.

Although it is beyond the scope of this book to train our readers how to raise financial support, let us offer just a few suggestions.

1. Bivocational church planting. The art of juggling two jobs is quickly becoming the norm, not the exception, in church-starting ventures. As time-consuming as it is to launch a new church, the reality is most church planters will have to finance their own way for a year or more, and many elect to hold a second job to support their ministry.

2. Missionary support raising. Although this can be a time-consuming task, a number of church planters are soliciting funds in the form of monthly pledges from their friends, family, col-

leagues, churches, and their denomination in order to embark on the work of church starting.

3. Sell the church building to support a new venture. This isn't as crazy as it sounds. We're not yet up to "many churches are selling their buildings," but we are aware of several new emerging church starts that have been financially supported by the sale of a building or property in order to launch something completely different. With church buildings eating up as much as 40 to 65 percent of a church's budget, many emerging churches are opting out of the real estate business.

4. Consider embracing a zero-based or other low-cost church-planting model. Not all church plants are expensive. Every Christian could launch a house church in their home for little or no cost. And a zero-based ministry is often easier to fund through grants or gifts than a straight church plant.

Having the funds to launch a church, however, isn't the same as having the funding to sustain a church plant. Depending on the model, church planting can be an expensive enterprise. Before launching out with a new church start, make sure you have plans to carry the weight of expenses for several years.

Other Pitfalls of the Emerging Church

What's the difference between shooting yourself in the foot and shooting yourself in the head? In one case you die, in the other you survive. Good church-planting coaches will do everything they can to keep their charge from suicide; however, many a good coach will warn, but not necessarily stop, church planters from shooting themselves in the foot. This last section is our attempt at warning our readers and colleagues of some of the potential, typically nonlethal, shots that can leave church leaders and their churches with a severe limp.

1. *Make up your mind.* Most of our under-the-radar churches are rather small and the leadership team relatively limited. That's not necessarily a bad thing (in fact, in our opinion, a streamlined team-based leadership team of five members or so is an ideal size), but it does allow for some significant mind changing as time goes by. Now, it's okay to change your mind, especially when

something isn't working, but several of these under-the-radar churches could be accused of changing their minds as often as the tides change in the ocean. Some leaders seem to change their minds about where they're going or how they're going to get there every time they read the newest book that hits the market. (We have to wonder what will happen when this one gets in their hands!) Others change their tactics every week: last week's servant evangelism project is dropped for today's focus group, which may be replaced by podcasting next week. Leaders who change their mind too often lose credibility, and their followers stop following. When that happens, forward motion grinds to a halt.

2. *The abuse of the copyright laws.* Napster wasn't the first corporate body guilty of widespread copyright violations. The church was. For years now it has been deemed essentially OK by church leaders for the music director to steal money from artists, writers, and publishers by illegally copying music for their church choirs or bands. With the rise of technology, the new emerging churches are finding it easier than ever to engage in thievery. In several of the churches we visited we couldn't help noticing the unauthorized use of altered and unaltered video clips, music not covered under the CCLI (Christian Copyright Licensing International) license agreements, copyrighted images, and clips from broadcast television. Although it is quite affordable for even the smallest of churches to buy a CCLI license that covers most, but not all, Christian music or a CVLI (Video) license that covers many, but not *nearly* all, video sources (and does *not* cover *any* broadcast material), many churches simply skip the licenses or else use music and film that is not covered. For instance, we have been to a number of churches where we've watched Harrison Ford take that fateful step onto nothingness in *Indiana Jones and the Last Crusade* or clips from a *Star Wars* movie. However, Lucasfilms does not allow churches (or much of anyone else) to use clips from its movies. But that hasn't stopped very many of us. The fact is, if the church is guilty of this, its integrity is in question. The world is just looking for chinks in our spiritual armor, and we don't need to give them another shot.

3. *Lack of accountability.* Many leaders are boiling in hot water because they have exhibited a lack of accountability. The problem is, with many of these under-the-radar churches, there is

no one to hold these women and men accountable to their own vision, mission, and values. Many church planters have Myers-Briggs NF personalities, which means they make decisions from the heart. However, the heart isn't always all that reliable and is subject to change—especially if the NF is coupled with a P. By engaging in an accountability partnership, the church planter is more likely to stay on task and on target with where they are called to go. There are many ways to achieve accountability, but one of the best ways is to hire a church-planting coach or a life coach who understands the pressures and dynamics of church planting. By meeting regularly with their coach, new church planters can see what is distracting them or identify when they have strayed from their plan.

Conclusion

Both of us believe that these under-the-radar churches have real potential as models for the future. Which ones will last and which ones won't may well depend on how they deal with issues we've posed above. Shooting yourself in the head is almost always fatal. A lack of evangelism results in a dying organization that we're not sure can even be called a church. The lack of a charismatic leader can result in an undersized church that either cannot grow or cannot sustain the growth it gets. The lack of strategic mapping—well, my (BTB) father always said, "If you aim at nothing, you'll hit it every time." And, the lack of financial planning generally results in broken hearts and broken banks.

On the other hand, if you only shoot yourself in the foot, you may survive. Heed the warnings and, though we won't promise you smooth sailing, we will promise there will be a couple of snares that you will avoid.

Take Two

• Evangelism is a lost art in many, if not most, of our churches today. How important is evangelism to your church? You can tell by looking at your church's annual budget and its calendar.

How much money is being set aside for outreach projects that result in souls coming to Jesus—not money sent to the denomination for missions and not mission support, but how much is being used within and by the local church to reach local residents? Then look to see how many of your calendared activities are targeted toward the unchurched. Don't count your worship service unless it is specifically targeting the unchurched (here's a hint, if you're still using a hymnbook or if you're singing songs written more than thirty years ago, you're not focusing on the unchurched). When you have those two bits of information, you're ready to discuss the question, *how important is evangelism to your church?*

• A related issue to the above paragraph is your personal value of evangelism. How much time do you spend in conversations with non-Christians? How much time dreaming up ways to connect with them? How much time equipping your leaders to share their faith? In many churches the average person in the pew is unprepared to share their faith. In some cases we've found pastors who are either reluctant or unwilling to share their faith. However, we've discovered that if you are a Christian and if you can effectively answer one particular question, then you are nearly ready to share. The question? *What is it about your relationship with Jesus that your neighbor can't live without?*

• Very few churches have a strategic map as a guide to achieving their vision by accomplishing their mission. Begin by asking around, what is your church's mission? If the folks in the congregation can't repeat it verbatim, then it's probably ineffective as a guiding principle. If you can't remember it, you've hardly internalized it. Next, ask what is your church's vision; where are you going as a church? If the vision isn't measurable, how will you know when you've reached it and need to reenvision? Once you know your church's mission and vision, consider what part you are playing in achieving them. Finally, how would your church be helped by a written strategic plan that was adopted by the congregation as whole?

• Most churches pride themselves in their ethical behavior; that is, we've never come across a church that has confessed they are unethical. And yet, they tend to gloss over some of the tough questions such as: (1) Does the church tolerate bullies who wield their power of personality or position to get their own way (in worship wars, financial decisions, mission or vision derailment, and so on)? If so, why? What does the church's response say about how the church views accountability? (2) Does the church tolerate the abuse of copyright laws? If so, how does the church justify it? Who is it stealing from?

CHAPTER TEN

HISTORY WILL BE
THE JUDGE

Well, have you decided? Is the Holy Spirit speaking to us in this book or are the authors full of hot air? Will any of these types of churches begin to show up on Christianity's radar screen? Are there any patterns in any of these examples that might become a trend in the decades ahead?

I think all of us would agree that the churches we have highlighted are different from the traditional churches of modernity, even the more contemporary baby boomer/praise type churches with all the multimedia. However, I doubt if we would find much consensus among the readers as to whether any of them represent the emerging church when it reaches maturity. These expressions of the emerging church are too new and too immature to say which one, if any, will set the course of the new world.

Our guess is that the future may not produce just one or two models of the emerging church as was true throughout most of modernity. We believe that diversity will be the hallmark of the emerging church. It certainly is at this point in time, and we are fully convinced that it will become the dominate shape of the emerging church.

Shared Characteristics

However, we do see some common characteristics in these churches we've chosen to examine that might give us some clues to the future church. It just may be that the commonalities found in these examples will ultimately point the way to the emerging church.

Conventional Wisdom Is Ignored

Each of these churches intentionally chose an untried path, not because they wanted to be different but because they had a spiritual itch they wanted to scratch. Some wanted to reach a segment of the population that was virtually untouched. Others simply wanted to do "their thing" and develop a church that fit their personality.

Most of them were considered too radical and too much of a risk for a denomination to support in any way so they set out on their own. A glance at history shows that most of the leaders of yesterday's movements were considered to be the mavericks of their day.

Everything Is Decentralized

Because Christianity lost its privileged position in society, it has been forced to decentralize its ministry and mission in order to penetrate a fractured, alienated, and hostile society. Whereas traditional churches offered the come-grow-with-us approach to mission, the emerging church asks people to be the church in the world.

Rather than just studying and/or using culture, these churches immerse themselves in it, not just rubbing shoulders with it, but actually living within it 24-7. By living within the culture, these churches bring their Jesus-influence with them, thus providing an opportunity for Christianizing the culture rather than trying to be an island of Christianity locked into an organized structure and protected *from* culture. These groups of Christians don't withdraw from the culture once a week to "do worship." Instead, worship is an adjective that describes how they teach their people to live all week as they live within the culture they are immersed in. We expect to see more and more of these pastors working a secular job and living a disciple's life in the market place as they engage in one-on-one discipleship with those around them.

These churches have replaced "going to meetings" with "leaving to serve and witness." Mission replaces meetings. People gain authority and power not by what committee they chair but by how they serve—something unheard of in most of the churches of modernity.

The ministry and mission of these churches is indigenous to the microcultures surrounding them. The standard baby boomer praise service with music, video, and sermon is replaced with a variety of off-the-wall attempts to reach deep into segments of society and speak to their specific needs. The phrase "order of worship" has little meaning. The life and character of the emerging church is being forged by the culture around it rather than the brand of a denomination or association. These churches are highly focused on reaching outside of their own membership, something a lot of churches talk about but few actually do.

Permission-giving environments and servant-empowering ministries always follow decentralization. The drive for power and control so endemic in modern churches is being replaced with ministries that bubble up from the gifts and interests throughout the congregation. People who function in such an environment do so out of love and respect more than duty or obligation.

However, decentralization comes with a down side: the loss of structure. Whereas the greatest threat to the modern church is bureaucracy, the loss of structure is the greatest threat to the emerging church. This loss of structure makes it more difficult for any sustained movement to emerge—another reason for saying that diversity will be the hallmark of the emerging church.

If this lack of structure is overcome, it will be due to the rise of ordered disciplines within these communities (more on this later). We already see these groups replacing organizational structure with an emphasis on personal order and discipline. Authority for the emerging leaders is based more on their effective and authentic relationships and accomplishments rather than denominational brand, hierarchical structure, personal piety, or academic degrees.

Multiple Communities Are Valued

In order to penetrate the culture, these churches find it necessary to develop multiple communities spread throughout the culture. Cell groups are foundational in almost all of these churches.

We're not talking about small groups as most people think of them. Cell groups are much more than Serendipity groups, or the kind of small groups that were part of the 40 Days of Purpose (as great as they were), or small groups that are part of some Lenten program.

Cell groups and/or house groups are life transformational to the point that they define the way people actually live out their day-to-day faith. They are as important as family. For many, they are an extended family. But in every case they are people forming significant relationships within and outside of the Christian community.

We feel that both the cell group and house church movements will continue to grow and become essential parts of the twenty-first-century landscape. Likewise, we feel the megachurch phenomenon of the past twenty years has peaked or soon will peak. One can only wonder if the postmodern crowd will support these huge structures or if the leadership will be comfortable serving in such environments. An examination of the Third World reveals thriving cell and house church movements. When society turns against Christianity, as we see it beginning to do in the United States, the institutionally based church suffers while the cell and house church thrives.

Ministry Is Redefined

The line of demarcation between clergy and laity is blurred almost to the point that it has little value anymore. Many of these church leaders have shrugged off any sort of organized church in order to build congregations built on relationships and participation. Just as these pastors aren't called to "THE ministry" but are called to follow Jesus just like any other Christian, the same is true for everyone in the congregation. Wholehearted participation is expected from everyone. They depend on the input of the congregation as a whole, not just a select few. Additionally, most of these churches value art and/or the creativity of the laity.

This view goes far beyond the stereotyped priesthood of the believer that we see in even some of the finest megachurches of today. It puts the final nail in the coffin of the clergy/laity distinction. The day of the professional hit-man view of the clergy is ending in these churches as ministry and spiritual living becomes the goal of all of the committed participants. Sometime in this century we expect to see either the end of official ordination of clergy or every gift of the church will have the hands or ordination laid on it. The clergy/laity distinction will not be upheld in the emerging church.

Niche Ministries Are Preferred

Instead of trying to become everything to everyone, these churches have chosen to focus on a niche. Doing so, allows them to do well what they do. We expect to see the rise of more churches that focus on niche ministries. The downside of niche ministries (if it can be considered a downside) is that these churches necessarily reach smaller crowds. By choosing to focus on one population or another, these churches choose not only whom they will reach but also whom they will *not* reach.

Personal Order and Discipline Are Central

These churches expect faith to be a seven-day-a-week relationship around which one's whole life revolves.[1]

We expect to see more emphasis placed on personal piety, journaling, devotional life, and monastic type of environments. No more Bible study just for the sake of mere learning. Today, mission is the reason to study the Bible: to learn how and what to do with one's life and ministry in the real world. Once again, discipleship takes on the shape of a student learning a trade (to be like Jesus) rather than an academic learning exercise from a book. This will necessitate the rise of the apprenticeship and mentoring models of training new disciples, a more relational way of being church to be sure.

It is only natural then that the leadership we see in these churches is organic. Most of these leaders function like gardeners.[2] Their role is to create a nurturing environment in which people are welcomed, transformed, equipped, and empowered to do God's will rather than fulfill the needs of the institutional church. What we have seen in these leaders is a far cry from the typical pastor who spends endless hours each year begging people to fill organizational slots in the institution and raising money to keep the wheels turning, often never venturing out into the real world nor ever helping a person find his or her way from darkness to light!

How Goes It?

So, here we are at the end of our journey into what might be the future. The churches of the twenty-first century will look nothing like the churches we see facing the county seat courtyards of yesteryear (or today, for that matter). You've been introduced to several of them.

- What did you see that excited you—or terrified you—as you read?
- What did you see that gave you a spiritual itch you feel compelled to scratch?
- And what are you going to do to scratch it?

NOTES

Preface

1. Bill Easum first described this crack in his book *Dancing with Dinosaurs*, published by Abingdon Press in 1993. He called it a "crack in history." What he described in that crack has come true beyond his wildest imagination.

1. What Is Church?

1. Acts 19:9-10: Paul took his disciples with him "and argued daily in the lecture hall of Tyrannus. This continued for two years, so that all the residents of Asia, both Jews and Greeks, heard the word of the Lord." The passage suggests that Paul rented the building in order to teach, lecture, and convince those who attended to become Christians. It is doubtful that this was anything like we understand as a church service.

2. Lest one think we are exaggerating, currently the fastest growing religious group in the United States is the unaffiliated—those who reject *all* religions. The next fastest growing religious group in terms of adherents is Islam. Geraldine Baum, "For Love of Allah," *Newsday* (Nassau and Suffolk Edition), part 2, March 7, 1989, p. 4. See also Ari L. Goldman, "Mainstream Islam Rapidly Embraced by Black Americans," *New York Times* (Late City Final Edition), February 21, 1989, p. 1.

3. Gallup Poll, May 2-4, 2004. Available at www.pollingreport.com/religion.htm (accessed June 8, 2004).

4. The term *mainline* is used to describe the group of denominations that were the "main" churches in the United States. These included the United Methodists, the Presbyterians, the Episcopalians, the Christian Church, and the Lutherans. Today, however, these denominations are all in serious decline from the past and no longer are in the majority. Indeed, some have stopped calling these denominations the mainline and have designated them the old-line.

5. From *kyrios*, Lord, and *oikia*, house. *Online Etymology*

111

Dictionary. Available at www.etymonline.com/index.php?1=c&p=13 (accessed July 25, 2003).

6. Definition from E. Cobham Brewer, *Dictionary of Phrase and Fable* (1898). Available at www.bartleby.com/81/3556.html (accessed July 25, 2003).

7. Numbers 20:8: "Take the staff, and assemble the congregation, you and your brother Aaron, and command the rock before their eyes to yield its water. Thus you shall bring water out of the rock for them; thus you shall provide drink for the congregation and their livestock."

8. Deuteronomy 4:9-11:

> But take care and watch yourselves closely, so as neither to forget the things that your eyes have seen nor to let them slip from your mind all the days of your life; make them known to your children and your children's children—how you once stood before the LORD your God at Horeb, when the LORD said to me, "Assemble the people for me, and I will let them hear my words, so that they may learn to fear me as long as they live on the earth, and may teach their children so"; you approached and stood at the foot of the mountain while the mountain was blazing up to the very heavens, shrouded in dark clouds.

9. Acts 9:2.

2. Attack of the Clones

1. Acts 8.

2. If this is indeed a new concept, we invite you to read *Dancing with Dinosaurs: Ministry in a Hostile and Hurting World* by Bill Easum (Nashville: Abingdon, 1993); Alan C. Klaas, *In Search of the Unchurched: Why People Don't Join Your Congregation* (Herndon, Va.: Alban Institute, 1996); and Tom Clegg and Warren Bird, *Lost in America: How You and Your Church Can Impact the World Next Door* (Loveland, Colo.: Group Publishing, 2001).

3. Psychographics are available from leading demographic and market research firms.

4. Felicity Dale, *Getting Started: Planting and Multiplying House Churches* (Austin: House2House, 2002), 102-4.

3. Common Ground, Seattle

1. http://dictionary.reference.com/search?q=indigenous.

2. www.forlovingkindness.org/julyaugust2002nsltr.html.

3. Romans 1:20.

4. Fred B. Craddock, *Overhearing the Gospel: Preaching and Teaching the Faith to Persons Who Have Already Heard* (Nashville: Abingdon, 1978). Craddock echoes Kierkegaard's indirect method as critical for the

authentic proclamation of the gospel. This method suggests there is something, says Gorsuch, "which one cannot directly communicate to the other" (Kierkegaard) and so must be revealed through story, metaphor, and (we would add) image. That something is the heart and soul of the gospel, which, in the words of Paul, is a mystery itself that we can only see dimly, as through a dark glass (1 Corinthians 13:12).

5. For more on this change, see Bill Easum, *Leadership on the OtherSide* (Nashville: Abingdon, 2000).

6. "Small Churches Struggle to Grow because of the People They Attract" (online article), *The Barna Update* (September 2, 2003), www.barna.org/FlexPage.aspx?Page=BarnaUpdate&BarnaUpdateID=148.

7. Jeremiah 31:33-34.

8. Hebrews 8:13.

9. Craddock, *Overhearing the Gospel*, 77.

4. Alpha Church

1. In May of 2004 the Church of England announced the creation of its first virtual parish and appointed its first webpastor. The purpose of the Internet church, or i-church, according to the Web site, "is to provide a Christian community for people who want to explore Christian discipleship but are not able to belong to a local congregation" (www.i-church.org/aboutichurch.php).

2. *Real time* is a computer term for this present moment. In a chat room this means you would see the message instantly, as opposed to e-mail, which can take some time to be delivered and can be perused at your convenience.

3. Web video cameras (webcams) provide a video feed to others who can view your image. This technology is still in its early development, so it is not yet as widely used as keyboard communications. However, webcams coupled with audio feeds will almost certainly replace keyboard chatting in the future.

4. A growing favorite forum is found at www.easumbandy.com within the EBA Community.

5. Larisa Thomason, "Promotion Tip: Query Your Visitors with Surveys" (online article), *NetMechanic* (April 2001), www.netmechanic.com/news/vol4/promo_no8.htm (accessed October 9, 2003).

6. Jacob Heller, "Holography: the Future of Digital Content Creation" (online article), *DCCCafe.com* (July 17, 2003), www.dcccafe.com/articles/article71703holograms.php (accessed October 9, 2003).

7. William Easum and Thomas G. Bandy, *Growing Spiritual Redwoods* (Nashville: Abingdon, 1997).

8. A PDA (personal digital assistant) is a hand-held device used for organizing and storing personal information.

9. Internet payment services such as Paypal.com offer an inexpensive way for offerings to be collected from the faithful.

10. Patricia Walker of Alpha Church submitted this brief response to our request for her thoughts about this chapter: "A family from Romania, writing in broken English, and a group of believers in Switzerland are our newest participants. It seems that once the church is discovered by just one person, then that person is likely to witness to their friends and family about the Good News available at any time of the day or night at AlphaChurch.org."

5. Imago Dei

1. Neil Cole, *Cultivating a Life for God* (Saint Charles, Ill.: ChurchSmart Resources, 1999).
2. Imagine the parents' appreciation too.
3. Stephen George and Arnold Weimerskirch, *Total Quality Management: Strategies and Techniques Proven at Today's Most Successful Companies* (The Portable MBA Series; 2nd ed.; New York: John Wiley & Sons, 1994), 16.

6. Greenhouse

1. Jonathan Chao, "Church Cooperation: A House Church Perspective" (online article), *World Evangelization Magazine* (n.d.), www.gospelcom.net/lcwe/wemag/9706chao.html (accessed April 1, 2004).
2. David Garrison, *Church Planting Movements* (Richmond, Va.: International Mission Board of the Southern Baptist Convention, 2000), 25.
3. Estimating the number of house churches in the United States is more hunch than science. There are some two thousand different Web addresses for U.S. house churches. Knowing that more house churches *don't* have Web sites than do and after ongoing discussions with many house church pastors and researchers, a guess of ten thousand or so is probably as accurate as any other guess.
4. Larry Kreider, *House Church Networks: A Church for a New Generation* (Ephrata, Pa.: House to House Publications, 2001), 2.
5. "Region: Macedonia...Prefecture: Thessaloniki" (online article), *Grecian Net* (n.d.), www.grecian.net/GREECE/macedonia/thessaloniki/thessaloniki.htm (accessed April 10, 2004).
6. Barbara Nield, "China's House Churches" (online article), *Renewal Journal* 3 (94:1), www.pastornet.net.au/renewal/journal3/neild.html (accessed April 10, 2004).
7. "Church Planting in India Update: Oct 2003" (online article), www.house2house.tv/index.pl/00054 (accessed April 10, 2004).
8. Sheryl Montgomery Wingerd, "News/Briefs" (online article), *DAWN Report* (July 2003), www.dawnministries.org/resources/dawn_report/issue51/news_briefs.html (accessed April 10, 2004).
9. Chris Turner, "Church: Where the Home Is" (online article), *TConline.org* (March 2002), http://archive.tconline.org/stories/march02/ecuador.html (accessed April 23, 2004).

10. Kreider, *House Church Networks*, 40.

11. Garrison, *Church Planting Movements*, 18-20.

12. Using a round number of 40 million relocations annually (from a 2000 U.S. census report) and the 84 percent of Americans who claim Christianity as their faith according to the Pew Research Center (data collected from www.adherents.com/rel_USA.html; Carol Faber, "Moving Rate Among Americans Declines, Census Bureau Says" (online article), *U.S. Census Bureau News* (January 19, 2000), www.census.gov/Press-Release/www/releases/archives/popula tion/000420.html (accessed March 22, 2005).

13. Wolfgang Simson, *Houses That Change the World: The Return of the House Churches* (Carlisle, England: Paternoster, 2001), 106-7.

7. The Rock House Church Network

1. Bill Tenny-Brittian, *The House Church Pastor Training Workbook* (Renton, Wash.: HouseNet Resources, 2004), 1.

2. Wolfgang Simson, *House Church Network Pastor's Seminar* (Vancouver, BC, November 17, 2003). Actually, the number approaches twelve million people, but for most of us that number is unfathomable, so we just left it at "literally millions."

3. See chapter 6, "Greenhouse," for Neil Cole's house church story.

4. Graduates of the House Church Seminary receive a diploma that is recognized only within the confines of The Rock House Church Network.

8. Zero-Based Ministry

1. I (BE) have written two articles that reinforce this shift and give concrete examples of actual churches. These articles are titled "What We Can Learn From America's Fastest-Growing Churches." They can be found in the EBA Community section of our Web site at www.easum bandy.com/community/articles.html?a=billeasum.

9. Why Some Under-the-Radar Churches Will Go the Way of the Wind

1. For more on strategic mapping go to http://easumbandy .com/store/shop/EBA_store.html then search the store for "strategic mapping."

10. History Will Be the Judge

1. For an excellent review of how many of these Third World churches are instilling the discipled life, see David Garrison's *Church Planting Movements* (Richmond, Va.: International Mission Board of the Southern Baptist Convention, 1999).

2. To read more about organic leadership see Bill Easum, *Leadership on the OtherSide* (Nashville: Abingdon, 2000).